Seven Things You Have To Know To Understand End Times Prophecy

By Jack Kelley

xulon PRESS

*7 Things You Have To Know To Understand
End Times Prophecy*
by Jack Kelley

Printed in the United States of America

ISBN 9781619043985

www.xulonpress.com

Dedication

This book is dedicated first and foremost to Our Lord Jesus by Whom and about Whom these prophecies are written, and second to my wife Samantha who has always been a loving and supporting helpmate, partner in ministry, and best friend.

About The Author

B efore retiring into full time ministry, Jack Kelley was a successful management consultant with clients throughout the Western US and Canada. Since that time he has devoted his time and energy to studying and teaching the Bible, and serving as teacher, counselor, and lay pastor. He has led several pilgrimages to Israel and Jordan, visiting New Testament sites in Turkey and Greece as well.

Jack is the author of all the articles on the ministry's website, www.gracethrufaith.com. These articles and his answers to questions on the Bible have been read by pastors, teachers and students in over 180 countries and territories around the world and are regularly used as sermon topics and Sunday School lessons as well. This has made gracethrufaith. com one of the world's most popular Bible Study websites,

Jack and his family currently reside on the Baja Peninsula in Mexico where they also serve as volunteer missionaries in the local community.

Introduction

With all the killer storms, earthquakes, wars and disease dominating our news, it's not surprising that people are becoming more interested in End Times Prophecy. Even non-believers are wondering if the end is near. What is surprising is how little most Christians actually know about end times prophecy, especially since by some accounts it comprises nearly 30% of the Bible's content, more than any other topic.

With few exceptions seminaries don't teach it, so preachers don't preach it. And therefore Christians don't learn it. In all my years as a denominational Christian, I never once heard a message explaining the importance of prophecy to a believer's walk with the Lord. And yet the Bible devotes more space to End Times Prophecy than it does to all the teachings of Jesus.

When Christians are asked why they don't study prophecy more seriously the most common reasons given are 1) because it scares them, and 2) because it confuses them. Both responses are borne out of a lack of understanding. For the believer, prophecy is neither scary nor confusing but the key to understanding God's plan for man.

The purpose of this book is to provide a solid foundation for further study. When the foundation of a building is stable and solid, the entire building is stronger, able to withstand powerful forces that would otherwise weaken or even topple it. So it is when the foundation of our study is solid. Powerful arguments from scoffers and unbelievers cannot shake us or weaken our faith. Let's get started.

Seven Things You Have To Know

There are seven pieces of information that are essential to understanding End Times Prophecy. These seven things are the building blocks for the strong foundation we want. They are,

1) The Sequence of Major End Time Events,
2) The Destiny of the Three Components of Humanity,
3) The Purpose and Length of the Great Tribulation,
4) The Purpose of the Rapture,
5) The Conditions Surrounding the 2nd Coming,
6) The Purpose and Length of the Millennium, and
7) Eternity.

Once you've learned them, these seven things will help you avoid the mistakes that have thrown others off the track. Call it perspective or overview or whatever you want, this combination of facts will

give you the ability to put all the prophetic verses in
the Bible into their proper context.

1

The Sequence Of Major End Times Events

Irst is knowing what happens and when. The study of prophecy gets really confusing if you don't know the sequence in which major End Times events will occur. Actually their order is very logical, and once you learn it, you'll wonder why you didn't see it before.

The best way to figure it out is to perform what the business world sometimes calls a back scheduling exercise. It involves going to the very end of a process and identifying the final outcome. Then you list all the things that have to happen to produce that outcome. Then you put them in reverse order, backing into the present. It's simpler than it sounds, and much simpler in prophecy than in business because there are many fewer events to organize. We'll list the major events first, then we'll organize them.

Almost everyone knows about the 2nd Coming and Eternity, and many also have heard of the Rapture of the Church and the Great Tribulation. But there's also the Millennial Kingdom, Daniel's 70th Week, and the Battles of Ezekiel 38-39, Psalm 83 and Isaiah 17; a total of nine major events yet to come. Now let's organize them, beginning with the final outcome and working back toward the beginning. As it is with most lists, the order in which some events will occur is obvious while others are less so, and at first some don't seem to fit any place at all. We'll order the obvious ones first.

What Are We Waiting For?

We all think of Eternity as the final outcome, and so starting at the end means we begin there. But the last major event described in any detail in the Bible is the Kingdom Age or Millennium. It's the Lord's 1000 year reign on Earth, which is distinguished from and precedes Eternity. The very last chapter of Revelation describes trees on either side of the River of Life bearing a different fruit every month (**Rev. 22:1-2**). That means time still exists, and Eternity by definition is the absence of time. We'll talk more about that later. For now let's just say that Eternity can't happen till the Millennium is over.

The Millennium obviously can't begin till after the Second Coming, because that's when the Lord returns to establish it. And according to **Matt. 24:29-30** the Second Coming won't happen till the end of the Great Tribulation. And that can't happen till the anti-Christ stands in the Temple in

Israel declaring himself to be God. (**2 Thes. 2:4**) That's the event Jesus warned Israel to look for as the Great Tribulation's opening salvo. He called it "The Abomination of Desolation" in **Matt. 24:15-21. Daniel 9:27** indicates it will happen in the middle of the last seven year period, which scholars call Daniel's 70th Week. (See Appendix 1 at the back of the book for a complete commentary on Daniel's 70th Week.)

But the Abomination can't happen until there's a Temple. There hasn't been a Temple in Israel since 70AD and there won't be one until the Jews officially decide they need one. They won't need one until God reinstates their Old Covenant relationship because the Temple's only purpose is to worship Him according to Old Covenant requirements.

This will signal the beginning of Daniel's 70th week. The 70th Week can't begin until the Battle of **Ezekiel 38-39** is won because God will use that battle to awaken Israel and reinstate His covenant with them (**Ezekiel 39:22**). In **Romans 11:25** Paul said Israel has been hardened in part until the full number of Gentiles has come in, a reference to the rapture of the Church, after which Israel will be saved. That means the rapture has to happen before the Battle of **Ezekiel 38**. (Appendix 2 contains a detailed explanation of **Ezekiel 38-39**)

You Got That?

So far when we put the Sequence of Major Events in its proper order, it looks like this:

The Rapture of the Church,
The Battle of Ezekiel 38,
Daniel's 70th week begins,
The Great Tribulation,
The 2nd Coming,
The Millennium,
Eternity.

To those who read Scripture as it's written, only two of the events in this sequence are subject to debate as to timing. These are the Rapture of the Church and the Battle of **Ezekiel 38**, the first two on our list. They're the ones I said are less obvious.

So lets find out why they have to be where I've placed them in the sequence. Maintaining our back schedule mentality, we'll begin with Ezekiel's battle and work back to the Rapture.

"And I will set my glory among the nations, and all the nations shall see my judgment that I have executed, and my hand that I have laid on them. The house of Israel shall know that I am the LORD their God, from that day forward.

Then they shall know that I am the LORD their God, because I sent them into exile among the nations and then assembled them into their own land. I will leave none of them remaining among the nations anymore. And I will not hide my face anymore from them, when I pour out my Spirit upon the house of Israel, declares the Lord GOD." (**Ezek 39:21-22, 28-29**)

The Lord has declared in no uncertain terms that He's going to use Ezekiel's battle to spiritually awaken His people and call them to Israel from all over the world. This will result in the reinstatement of their Old Covenant relationship, reviving Daniel's long dormant "70-Weeks" prophecy for its final seven years and requiring that a Temple be constructed. Without one there's no way for them to keep His covenant.

This was proven once before in history during the Babylonian captivity. When Nebuchadnezzar destroyed the 1st Temple, Israel ceased to exist. But as soon as Cyrus the Persian defeated Babylon and freed the Jews, they returned to Israel and began building a Temple before they did anything else. Without a Temple there's no sacrifice for sin, and without that sacrifice, Jews cannot approach God.

Both the Old and New Testaments refer to a Temple in Israel at the End of the Age. The only reason for a Temple is to perform Old Covenant ordinances. But building one today would cause such an uproar that no one in his right mind would consider it.

Only a unified demand from the people of Israel accompanied by quiet acceptance from their Moslem neighbors would make the construction of a Temple even thinkable. Sound impossible? Ezekiel's battle results in both a Jewish nation re-awakened to the presence of God in their national life and an utterly defeated Moslem attack force in no position to resist. The perfect conditions will finally exist to start building. For these reasons, Ezekiel's battle has to take place on the threshold of Daniel's 70th week. Now why does the Rapture of the Church have to precede Ezekiel's battle?

Lest you be wise in your own conceits, I want you to understand this mystery, brothers: a partial hardening has come upon Israel, until the fullness of the Gentiles has come in. (**Romans 11:25**)

According to **Ezek. 37:7-10**, Israel would be reborn first in unbelief. Paul said they'll remain partially estranged from God until the gentile Church reaches its full complement (predetermined number) and arrives at its destination. (The Greek word translated "fullness" in **Romans 11:25** was a nautical term often used to describe the full complement of crew and cargo necessary to accomplish a ship's mission. The ship couldn't sail till those requirements were met. The one translated "come in" means to arrive at a designated place.)

Then the veil will be pulled back as God reveals Himself to them again. As we saw above, He will use Ezekiel's battle to begin this by renewing the Old Covenant with them, later transitioning Israel from the Old Covenant to the New toward the end of the Great Tribulation (**Zech 12:10**). Remember, if they didn't go back to the Old covenant first, they wouldn't need a Temple. He's picking them up where they left off.

After they finished speaking, James replied, *"Brothers, listen to me. Simeon has related how God first visited the Gentiles, to take from them a people for his name. And with this the words of the prophets agree, just as it is written,*

'After this I will return, and I will rebuild the tent of David that has fallen; I will rebuild its ruins, and I will restore it, that the remnant of mankind may seek the Lord, and all the Gentiles who are called by my name, says the Lord, who makes these things known from of old.' (**Acts 15:13-18**)

It was about 20 years after the cross. The controversy of the day was whether Gentiles had to become Jews before they could become Christians. And if not, what would become of Israel? In effect, the Lord's brother James explained to the Apostles and others present at the Council of Jerusalem that Israel was being temporarily set aside while God focused on the Church. After He had taken this "people for His name" (Christians) from among the Gentiles he would return and rebuild His Temple. The Greek words translated taken means to carry something away or remove it from its place, so the passage implies that He would take the Church somewhere and then come back to rebuild the Temple, restore Israel, and give what's left of mankind one final chance to seek Him.

These three Bible prophecies make it clear that as the End of the Age approaches, God will begin preparing Israel to be His once more. But He won't be exclusively focused on them until He has finished building the Church and has taken us to our appointed place. And where is that?

In my Father's house are many rooms; if it were not so, I would have told you. I am going there to prepare a place for you. And if I go and prepare a place for you, I will come back and take you to be with me that you also may be where I am. (**John 14:2-3**)

He didn't promise to come back to be with us here where we are, but to take us there, where He is. After that He would see to Israel's reawakening and the construction of their Temple.

Throughout Scripture, the Lord seems to be involved with either Israel or the Church, but never both at the same time. James bears this out in his pronouncement regarding the Church in **Acts 15**. All the leaders of the early church now knew that once God had accomplished His goals with the church, He would turn again to Israel, and that would signal the end of the Church Age.

There are two critical points to remember here. The first is that the Church didn't end God's covenant with Israel, but only interrupted it 7 years short of its scheduled completion. Those seven years, called the 70th Week of Daniel, have to be fulfilled to complete the Old Covenant.

And the second is that the Old and New covenants, as practiced in Israel and the Church, are theologically incompatible, and therefore the two can only be on Earth at the same time while Israel is out of covenant. For Israel to return to the Lord, the Church has to be gone.

For this reason, the rebirth of Israel in 1948 and the reunification of Jerusalem in 1967 are seen as the most important signs of all that the End of the Age is upon us.

Also, there are two events we haven't put into the sequence yet, and that's because they aren't easy to locate there. These are the battles of **Psalm 83** and **Isaiah 17**. When Israel wins these two battles all their next door enemies will be defeated and they'll enter into a brief period of peace that sets the stage for Ezekiel's Battle (**Ezekiel 38:11**). They're called battles instead of wars which means they'll be of short duration and can happen within a fairly short span of time. They can come either before or after the Rapture but do have to happen before the Battle of **Ezekiel 38** takes place. (**Psalm 83** is explained in Appendix 3 and **Isaiah 17** follows in Appendix 4)

2

The Destiny Of The Three Components Of Humanity: The Nations (aka Gentiles), Israel, And The Church

E ven so-called experts misinterpret prophecy when they don't stop to consider who the Lord, or one of His prophets, is addressing. Just because something's in the Gospels doesn't necessarily mean that it's for the Church, or being in Isaiah that it's only for Israel. Knowing a prophecy's intended recipient is critical to understanding it, and there are three possibilities. I'll show you what I mean.

His purpose was to create in himself one new man out of the two, thus making peace, and in this one body to reconcile both of them to God through the cross, by which he put to death their hostility. (**Ephes. 2:15-16**)

Do not cause anyone to stumble, whether Jews, Greeks (Gentiles) *or the church of God.* (**1 Cor. 10:32**)

You are all sons of God through faith in Christ Jesus, for all of you who were baptized into Christ have clothed yourselves with Christ. There is neither Jew nor Greek, slave nor free, male nor female, for you are all one in Christ Jesus. (**Galatians 3:26-28**)

In the 4,000 or so years from the Creation to the Cross, the human race came to be divided into three distinct components from God's perspective. Here's how it happened. From the Creation there was one race of Humans, the family of man, later called Gentiles, or Nations.

Then in **Genesis 12**, God called Abraham to build a great nation to be separate from the others. He and his descendants were first called Hebrews (**Genesis 14:13**), and later Jews (**Ezra 4:12**). From that time on, the world's population was either Jew or Gentile.

But at the cross God created the Church, taken from among both Jews and Gentiles but sharing a destiny with neither. Now there were three, and everyone on Earth belongs to of one of them. In his epistles, Paul always took pains to distinguish the Church from both Jews and Gentiles, in effect calling the Church a new race of Human in the passages I cited above. I'll describe each group's destiny so you can see how different they are.

First the Gentiles. According to **Isaiah 56:6-8**, Gentiles who converted to Judaism before the cross became part of Israel and share its destiny (see below) as long as they died in faith of a coming Redeemer. Gentiles who are born again during the Church Age become part of the church and after the rapture / resurrection will populate the New Jerusalem (**Rev. 21**). Many of us were taught to call it Heaven, but it's actually a separate entity. (More on this in our discussion of the Millennium, item 6 on our list of 7 Things You Have To Know.)

Gentiles who meet the Lord after the rapture are called tribulation believers. They're either martyred for their faith, in which case their spirits will go to serve God in His Temple (**Rev 17:13-17**) and will be joined with resurrection bodies at the time of the 2nd Coming (**Rev. 20:4**), or they'll survive the Great Tribulation to help re-populate the nations of Earth in the Kingdom age (Millennium).

Next the Jews. The spirits of Jews who died in faith of a coming redeemer before Jesus went to the cross were taken into Heaven with Him after His resurrection (**Matt. 27:52-53**). They'll also receive resurrection bodies at the Second Coming (**Daniel 12:1-3**). Jews who are born again during the Church age become part of the Church and after the rapture / resurrection will populate the New Jerusalem (**Rev. 21**). Jews who receive Jesus as their Messiah after the rapture will be hidden in the Jordanian desert (Petra) during the Great Tribulation. (**Rev. 12:14**) Along with their Old Testament counter parts they'll dwell in Israel during the Millennium. (**Ezekiel 43:6-7**)

Whether Jew or Gentile, those who don't do any of the above during their lifetimes will be tormented in Hell until they're brought back to life to stand trial at the Great White Throne judgment of **Revelation 20:11-15**. It takes place at the end of the Millennium. At that time, they'll be sentenced to eternal suffering in the Lake of Fire. (**Rev. 20:14**)

In the Old Testament, God promised Israel that He would return one day to dwell among them in their land on Earth forever (**Ezekiel 43:6-7**). In the New Testament, Jesus promised the Church that He would come back and take us to be with Him in His Father's House (**John 14:1-3**). Both promises come true. Israel is not the Church nor is the Church Israel, and both groups are distinct from the Gentile nations. Much of the confusion surrounding End Times prophecy results either from the failure to understand, or the refusal to accept, this truth.

For instance, many Christians today believe that the Church has replaced Israel in God's plan and has inherited all of Israel's blessings. Israel no longer serves any purpose in the world, they think, so when God talks about Israel in the New Testament He really means the Church. Therefore they misunderstand the Doctrine of Election, the Olivet Discourse, the Great Tribulation, and other New Testament teachings having to do with Israel.

Also, many Gentiles sit in pews on Sundays and think they're in the church even though they're not born again. They think they're saved because they try to live a good life, or give money, or belong to a particular denomination. They're wrongly convinced that the Church's blessings are theirs.

So there are three components of humanity and they all have different destinies. New Jerusalem is for the Church, Israel is for the Jews, and the rest of the world is for Gentile believers who will re-populate the Earth after the 2nd Coming. All surviving non-believers, whether Jew or Gentile, will be taken away at the time of the 2nd Coming to await the Great White Throne Judgment at the end of the Millennium with unbelievers of all ages.

3

The Purpose And Length Of
The Great Tribulation

How awful that day will be! None will be like it. It will be a time of trouble for Jacob, but he will be saved out of it. I am with you and will save you,' declares the LORD. 'Though I completely destroy all the nations among which I scatter you, I will not completely destroy you. I will discipline you but only with justice; I will not let you go entirely unpunished.' (**Jeremiah 30:7,11**)

J esus said that the Great Tribulation would be the most intense period of judgment the world has ever seen, greater than the World Wars, and even greater than the Flood of Noah. He said that if it were left to run its course, not a single human being would survive. But for the sake of His people He would stop it at its appointed time (**Matt. 24:22**).

The purpose of the Great Tribulation is two-fold. It's explained in the Jeremiah passage above, where it's called by its Old Testament name, the Time of Jacob's Trouble. God will use it to completely destroy the nations among whom His people have been scattered, and to discipline Israel, purifying them to dwell with Him in the Promised Land. The Church, having been purified at the cross, requires neither destruction nor discipline and has no business in the Great Tribulation.

(No matter where you place the Rapture in the End Times Scenario, if you believe in the Lord's all-sufficient work on the cross, then you know that the Church has to be protected from the End Times judgments, not purified by them. If you don't believe the Lord's work was sufficient, but that the coming judgments are needed to finish what He only began, then you have much bigger problems than figuring out when the Rapture will occur.)

The length of the Great Tribulation is variously given as 3 1/2 years (**Daniel 12:7**), 42 months (**Rev. 11:2**), or 1260 days (**Rev. 12:6**). If you use a 12 month 30 day calendar for a total of 360 days in a year, these three measurements all turn out to be the same length.

Some commentators claim that in **Matt. 24:22** Jesus said this time would be cut short, and the English translation does seem to imply this, but it has to be an incorrect interpretation of the Lord's intent. I say this because while **Daniel 12** was written several hundred years before the Lord spoke on the matter, John wrote Revelation 60 years after the resurrection. Therefore, it's length was made clear in testimony given both before the Lord's time and after it. If He said the Great Tribulation is going to be cut short then He contradicted both Daniel and John, something the Bible can't do. More likely the intent of **Matt. 24:22** is to explain that if the Lord doesn't return to put an end to the Great Tribulation at the appointed time no one would survive it, but for the sake of His elect He will return to put an end to it.

The 3 1/2 years, 42 months, 1260 days references lead us to believe that Earth's original calendar consisted of 12 months with 30 days each, and in fact it appears that prior to about 700 BC all the Earth used such a calendar. Since then a number of different calendars have emerged, apparently to compensate for changes that took place in the Earth's orbit about that time. (The calendar used by Western Nations today is only about four hundred years old.)

In addition, **Daniel 9:27** warns that an Abomination That Causes Desolation will occur in the middle of the last seven years, or 3 1/2 years from the end. In **Matt. 24:21** Jesus identified this event as the official beginning of the Great Tribulation. Paul confirmed this and added detail by describing the anti-Christ standing in the Temple proclaiming himself to be God. (**2 Thes. 2:4**) This confirms the length of the Great Tribulation as being 3 1/2 years.

The Abomination That Causes Desolation is a particular defilement of the Temple that's happened only once in history. In 168 BC. Syrian King Antiochus Epiphanes captured the Temple and converted it into a pagan worship center. He erected a statue of Zeus with his own face on it in the Holy Place, thereby proclaiming himself to be God, and demanded the Jews worship it on pain of death. It was called the Abomination That Causes Desolation because it made the Temple unfit for use and triggered the 3 1/2 year Maccabean Revolt. The Jewish re-capture and cleansing of the Temple in 165 BC is celebrated in the eight day Feast of Hanukkah.

To summarize, Daniel spoke of an Abomination That Causes Desolation that would mark the middle of the last 7 years. An event called the Abomination That Causes Desolation in 1st Maccabbees took place in 168 BC, over 300 years later. But 200 years after that, Jesus told His Disciples that the people of Israel should watch for a future Abomination That Causes Desolation and referred to Daniel's prophecy in doing so (**Matt. 24:15-21**). He said it would kick off the Great Tribulation. Paul also described a future event similar to the one in 168BC saying the "Day of the Lord" could not precede it (**2 Thes. 2:3-4**).

Therefore, the Abomination That Causes Desolation that took place in 168 BC was only a partial fulfillment of Daniel's prophecy. Jesus referred to it so people in end times would be able to recognize the complete fulfillment when they saw it. They'll know to look for a man standing in the Temple calling himself God and demanding that his image be worshiped. Jesus told those living in Judea (Israel) that when they see it to flee into hiding immediately, for the Great Tribulation will have begun. (You can read a detailed explanation of the Lord's explanation of End Times events in Appendix 5, called the Olivet Discourse.)

4

The Purpose Of The Rapture

They tell how you turned to God from idols to serve the living and true God, and to wait for his Son from heaven, whom he raised from the dead–Jesus, who rescues us from the coming wrath. (**1 Thes. 1:9-10**)

The Greek word translated from in the above passage is "apo." Literally it means to keep the subject (us) away from the time, place, or any relation to the event being referenced, in this case the coming wrath. This verse is one of several that explain the purpose of the Rapture of the Church, and that's to hide us safely out of the way before God visits His wrath upon the Earth. OK, but when does God's wrath come?

Then the kings of the earth, the princes, the generals, the rich, the mighty, and every slave and every free man hid in caves and among the rocks of the moun-

tains. They called to the mountains and the rocks, "Fall on us and hide us from the face of him who sits on the throne and from the wrath of the Lamb! For the great day of their wrath has come, and who can stand?" (**Rev 6:15-17**)

After **Revelation 3** the church is not seen on Earth again until we come back with the Lord in **Rev. 21:2**, as predicted in **Rev. 17:14**. In **Rev. 4** John sees a door standing open in heaven and is told to "Come up here!" Instantly he finds himself in the spirit, standing before the throne of God at the end of the age. He's been transported to the time of the Rapture.

He sees 24 elders there, seated on thrones of their own around the throne of God. They're all dressed in white with crowns of gold on their heads. They bow down before the Lord and place their crowns at his feet giving honor and glory to him. In chapter 5 they call themselves Kings and Priests as they sing praises to God. By their titles, clothing, crowns, thrones, and activities it's clear that they represent the newly raptured church.

There are four Old Testament views of the Throne of God. Those in Isaiah **6:1-4** and **Ezekiel 1** and **10** don't include these 24 elders. The one in **Daniel 7:9-10**, an end of the age vision, hints at multiple thrones but offers no detail. But in the Book of Revelation the 24 elders are mentioned 12 times. Some group has arrived in Heaven that wasn't there in Old Testament times, and 12 is the number of government. It's the Church, come to rule and reign with Christ.

So the Church is raptured in chapter 4, and is shown in heaven in chapter 5, while on Earth God's wrath is loosed in chapter 6 as the passage above clearly states.

Paul's first letter to the Thessalonians was written in 51AD and contains the very first clear mention of a Rapture ever given. Neither Jesus nor the Disciples ever taught it. Its existence was kept secret until then just as its exact timing is secret to this day. Many of the mistakes made about the timing of the rapture come from futile attempts to find Gospel passages that teach it, as we'll see in our discussion about the Second Coming.

In the church, we think the Rapture is perhaps the single most important component of End Times prophecy, and for us it is. So why didn't Jesus ever mention it? **1 Cor. 2:6-10** gives us the answer.

We do, however, speak a message of wisdom among the mature, but not the wisdom of this age or of the rulers of this age, who are coming to nothing. No, we speak of God's secret wisdom, a wisdom that has been hidden and that God destined for our glory before time began. None of the rulers of this age understood it, for if they had, they would not have crucified the Lord of glory. However, as it is written:

"No eye has seen, no ear has heard, no mind has conceived what God has prepared for those who love him" — but God has revealed it to us by his Spirit.

The phrase "rulers of this age" refers to Satan & Co. Had they known the astonishing abundance of blessings the Lord would shower down upon those who accept His death as payment for their sins, they would have done everything in their power to prevent the crucifixion.

Think of it. We're called Kings and Priests, given incalculable wealth and influence, made heirs with Christ of God's estate, something Satan could never achieve and we could never deserve, and it's all ours just because we believe. This realization came to Satan after it was too late to prevent it and turned what should have been his greatest victory into an agonizing defeat.

And having disarmed the powers and authorities, he made a public spectacle of them, triumphing over them by the cross. (**Colossians 2:15**)

But like everything in God's plan, you'll find hints of the Rapture even in the Old Testament. Look at this passage from **Isaiah 26:19-21**.

But your dead will live; their bodies will rise. You who dwell in the dust, wake up and shout for joy. Your dew is like the dew of the morning; the earth will give birth to her dead. Go, my people, enter your rooms and shut the doors behind you; hide yourselves for a little while until his wrath has passed by. See, the LORD is coming out of his dwelling to punish the people of the earth for their sins.

Notice how the pronouns change from second person when God speaks of His people to third person when He speaks of the people of the Earth. It means the two groups are different. One is told to hide because the other is going to be punished. (Note: the Hebrew word translated "go" in the phrase "Go my people" is translated "come" in some translations, recalling the command to John in **Revelation 4**, "Come up here!" But the word has another primary meaning and it's my favorite. It means vanish. "Vanish, my people!" Yes we will.)

Now read two of Paul's most popular Rapture disclosures.

According to the Lord's own word, we tell you that we who are still alive, who are left till the coming of the Lord, will certainly not precede those who have fallen asleep. For the Lord himself will come down from heaven, with a loud command, with the voice of the archangel and with the trumpet call of God, and the dead in Christ will rise first. After that, we who are still alive and are left will be caught up together with them in the clouds to meet the Lord in the air. And so we will be with the Lord forever. (**1 Thes 4:15-17**)

Now, brothers, about times and dates we do not need to write to you, for you know very well that the day of the Lord will come like a thief in the night. While people are saying, "Peace and safety," destruction will come on them suddenly, as labor pains on a pregnant woman, and they will not escape. But you, brothers, are not in darkness so that this day should surprise you like a thief. You are all sons of the light and sons of the day. We do not belong to the night or to the darkness. (**1 Thes. 5:1-5**) *For God did not appoint us to suffer wrath but to receive salvation through our Lord Jesus Christ.* (**1 Thes. 5:9**)

Here's another even more dramatic shift of pronouns. Using the third person, Paul describes unbelievers caught by surprise, thinking they had entered a period of peace as destruction suddenly rains down upon them, cutting off all hope of escape. Then Paul switched to the second person, telling believers we shouldn't be taken by surprise as the End approaches, and finally to the first person as he includes us with him, not appointed to wrath.

Now watch carefully as we lay Isaiah's writings over Paul's. *But your dead will live; their bodies will rise. You who dwell in the dust, wake up and shout for joy. Your dew is like the dew of the morning; the earth will give birth to her dead. (The dead in Christ will rise first.)*

Go, my people, enter your rooms and shut the doors behind you; hide yourselves for a little while until his wrath has passed by. (After that, we who are still alive and are left will be caught up together with them in the clouds to meet the Lord in the air.)

See, the LORD is coming out of his dwelling to punish the people of the earth for their sins. (While people are saying, "Peace and safety," destruction

*will come on them suddenly, as labor pains on a
pregnant woman, and they will not escape.)*

Although the Bible contains 66 books and
involved 40 writers, there's one Author and His message is consistent from Genesis through Revelation.
This is how Paul could open his passage on the rapture by saying, *"According to the Lord's own word
..."*. The Lord never mentioned the rapture in the
Gospels. Paul had read Isaiah.

Of course there are several more passages where
our Lord promises to protect us from the coming
judgments. And although the cynics can truthfully
say that the word rapture doesn't appear in any of
them, don't pay any attention to that. They're just
trying to confuse us.

They know that rapture is a word of Latin origin,
not Hebrew or Greek, the languages of the Bible. (The
earliest translation of the Bible was into Latin, and
the term rapture comes from there.) Its Greek equivalent is harpazo, which is found in the Greek text of
1 Thes. 4:15-17. When translated into English, both
words mean "to be caught up, or snatched away."

There's a similar situation with the word Lucifer,
also of Latin origin. It doesn't appear in any of the
original texts either, but no one would be naive
enough to deny the existence of Satan on such a
flimsy basis. (You can read more on why the Rapture
has to precede all of Daniel's 70th Week in Appendix
6.)

5

Conditions Surrounding
The 2nd Coming

A couple of days before He was arrested, Jesus had a private conversation with four of His disciples, His inner circle. They were Peter and Andrew, and James and John, two pair of brothers. The purpose of the conversation was to answer questions they had asked Him about the 2nd Coming and the End of the Age. They were confused because according to the prophecy of **Daniel 9:24-27** these events were only seven years away, and yet Jesus had just told them the Temple and all the surrounding buildings would be torn down so completely that not one stone would be left standing on another (**Matt. 24:1-2**). He had told the crowds the same thing on Palm Sunday and said it was going to happen because the nation hadn't recognized the time of His coming to them (**Luke 19:44**).

His response to the disciples' questions is contained in **Matt. 24-25**, **Mark 13**, and **Luke 21**. Theologians call it the Olivet Discourse because the conversation took place on the Mt. of Olives. For this study, we'll only summarize it, focusing on the parts that help us identify what the Lord had to say about the conditions surrounding the 2nd Coming. You can read a more detailed commentary on the Olivet discourse in Appendix 3 at the back of the book.

In Matthew's account, the most detailed, Jesus included several specific geographic and time references in His answer. He did this so His readers wouldn't get confused as to who and when He was talking about. Having commanded us to understand this passage in **Matt. 24:15**, He wanted to make sure we got it right. We'll use these references to get a clear understanding of His target audience and the timing of events.

His answer to their questions begins in **Matt. 24:4** with a general overview. He said false Messiahs would deceive many and that there would be wars and rumors of war, but they wouldn't be signaling the end. He characterized them, along with famines and earthquakes in various places, as the beginning of birth pangs. Birth pangs tell an expectant mother the labor and delivery are coming, but don't say exactly when they'll take place. It's the same with these signs.

He said they (the Jews) would be persecuted and put to death and hated by all nations, causing many to turn away from the faith and even betray each other, but those who stand firm to the end would be saved. Then He finished His summary in **Matt. 24:14**, saying the gospel would be preached in all nations and then the end would come. (According to **Rev. 14:6-7**, this prophecy will be fulfilled by an angel shortly after the Great Tribulation begins.)

"So when you see standing in the holy place 'the abomination that causes desolation,' spoken of through the prophet Daniel—let the reader understand— then let those who are in Judea flee to the mountains. (**Matt. 24:15-16**)

These two verses give us the first specific clues as to both the intended audience and the timing of His answer. The Holy Place is the Jewish Temple and as we learned in Part 2, the abomination that causes desolation is a specific defilement that makes it unfit for further use.

The last Temple to stand in Israel was destroyed in 70 AD before this prophecy could be fulfilled. The nation itself ceased to exist about 135 AD and didn't reappear until 1948. But because there's still no Temple there, the prophecy remains unfulfilled. Also it's directed to those who are in Judea, the Biblical name for Israel. The Lord was warning people in Israel who will be alive when a Temple is being built there to watch for this, and when they see it to flee immediately.

Pray that your flight will not take place in Winter or on the Sabbath. For then there will be a great tribula-

tion, such as has not occurred since the beginning of the world until now, nor ever will. (**Matt. 24:20-21**)

The mountains of Judea are treacherous in the winter, and Jews are forbidden under the Law to travel more than 1000 paces on the Sabbath for any reason. This confirms that the warning is intended for latter-day Israel, back in its Old Covenant relationship at the beginning of the Great Tribulation, 3 1/2 years from the Second Coming. The Church will already be gone.

Then in **Matt 24:29** He said that immediately after the tribulation ends, *the sun will be darkened, and the moon will not give its light; the stars will fall from the sky, and the heavenly bodies will be shaken.* When they see these signs they'll know that The Great Tribulation has ended.

Matt 24:30 has people on Earth seeing the Sign of the Son of Man in the sky, and then His visible return to Earth with power and great glory. This will cause all the peoples of the Earth to mourn. It's now too late for them to be saved and they intuitively realize it. This is the Lord's Second Coming.

Matt 24:36 begins with *"No one knows about that day or hour ..."* What day? What hour? According to Matt. **24:37** and **39** it's the day and hour of the Second Coming. Remember to stay in context. That's been His subject since verse 30. I believe the reason He said "day or hour" is so we would know for sure that He was talking about the actual day and hour of His Coming, not the general time. The specific timing of the 2nd coming is shrouded in mystery. No less than 4 times within a span of 27 verses Jesus said the people alive on Earth at the time will not know the day or hour of His coming in advance (**Matt. 24:36, 42-44, 50, Matt. 25:13**). In fact the only time He used the day and hour phrase was in conjunction with His 2nd Coming.

This lends support to the idea that the 2nd Coming will likely take place on the Feast of Trumpets. It was called the feast where no one knows the day or hour because it came on a new moon, which was very difficult to see in the night skies. Add to that the fact that immediately after the Great Tribulation the Moon will go dark entirely (**Matt. 24:29**) and it makes an already difficult task all but impossible.

Matt 25 begins with the phrase "At that time, ..." which is the time immediately following the 2nd Coming, and contains three illustrations the Lord used to describe judgments He'll conduct after He returns. I'll just high light what they reveal about the identity of their intended recipients.

The Parable of 10 Virgins

The first one is the Parable of 10 Virgins (**Matt. 25:1-13**). It's a story about 10 young women waiting for a bridegroom to come. All have oil lamps but because they've been waiting a long time, five have run out of oil and are trying to buy more when he arrives. Lacking oil they're denied entry into the Wedding Banquet. This parable is sometimes used to illustrate the precarious position of "backsliders" in the Church, but even if you disregard the problem with timing almost everything about that interpretation is wrong.

First, if oil is being used symbolically here, as I believe it is, then the principle of Expositional Constancy demands that it represent the Holy Spirit. This principle says that when things are used symbolically in Scripture, the symbolic use is consistent. For example yeast (leaven) always symbolizes sin, and oil always symbolizes the Holy Spirit. Can the Church lose the Holy Spirit, or exhaust our supply of Him? **Ephesians 1:13** and **2 Cor. 1:21-22** both say that the Holy Spirit has been sealed within us as a guarantee of our inheritance, and that it happened solely because we believed the Gospel message. There's nothing anyone anywhere can do to change that.

But no such guarantee is indicated for Tribulation believers. In fact **Rev. 16:15** specifically warns them to stay awake and maintain their righteousness, symbolized by keeping their clothes with them. (Clothing is often used to represent righteousness, as in **Isaiah 61:10**). **Rev. 16:15** implies that Tribulation believers are responsible for remaining steadfast in their faith to avoid losing their salvation. **Matt. 25:8** agrees, telling us that all 10 virgins had oil in their lamps at the beginning, but the five foolish ones didn't have enough to carry them through. Remember, all 10 virgins are caught sleeping when He returns. It's the oil that distinguishes one group from the other, not their behavior.

Second, these 10 women are called virgins or bridesmaids, but never the Bride. Conversely, the

Church is the Bride, and is never called a brides-maid! And when did you ever hear of a bride having to plead with the groom for admission to her own wedding banquet?

Third, it looks like these young women are trying to get into the Seudas Mitzvah (wedding feast) a ban-quet that follows the wedding ceremony. If so, none of them made it to the actual marriage ceremony, oil or not, so none of them can be the bride. In fact there's no bride mentioned anywhere in this parable.

These virgins aren't the Church. They represent Tribulation survivors trying to get into the Millennial Kingdom. Five were saved in the time between the Rapture and the end of the Great Tribulation (sig-nified by the oil), remained steadfast, and are wel-comed in. The five without oil when He arrived did not remain steadfast and lost their place.

This parable teaches that the Lord's return sig-nals the deadline after which even the request to be saved and receive the Holy Spirit will be denied. The door to the Kingdom will be closed, and the Lord will deny knowing those who've come too late.

The Parable Of The Talents

In **Matt 25:14**, at the beginning of the Parable of the Talents, the word "again" means he's giving another illustration from the same time period as the parable of the 10 Virgins, the Day of His Coming.

Though our use of talent as being a gift or ability derives from this parable, a talent was a Greek unit of measure, usually monetary. The key to interpreting a parable is knowing that everything is symbolic of something else, so in this parable a talent represents something valuable to the Lord that he wished to have invested on His behalf. Upon his return, He asks those to whom he had entrusted it what they've accomplished.

Those who teach that the talents are gifts given to the Church to be used wisely, producing a measurable return, haven't read the last verse of the parable. The servant who buried his talent in the ground and produced nothing with it was thrown into the outer darkness, the destiny of unbelievers. Is the Lord teaching a works based salvation here? Threatening us with the loss of our salvation if we don't produce enough with the gifts He gave us? Of course not.

Reading the Bible, it's clear that money isn't important to the Lord. But **Psalm 138:2** says that He values His Word above all else. I believe the talents represent His Word. Those who sow it into the hearts of others find that it multiplies in new believers. Those who study it find that their own understanding grows, multiplying their faith.

But those who ignore His word find that it's like burying it in the ground. Out of sight, out of mind, until what little they began with is lost to them. This proves it never held any value for them, and condemns them as unbelievers, to be cast into the outer darkness. They had heard the truth and ignored it. Now it's too late. In **2 Thes. 2:10** Paul describes them as those who perish because they refused to love the Truth and so be saved. Some will bear the further responsibility of having led their followers astray by their refusal to teach the truth.

In His Word, the Lord laid out every action He would take regarding His plan for Planet Earth. *"Surely the Sovereign LORD does nothing without revealing his plan to his servants the prophets,"* He said (**Amos 3:7**). He did this so man would never have to wonder what He was up to. And where the End of the Age is concerned He had more to say than about any other subject. No one can plead ignorance. Again the point is that some who survive the Great Tribulation will be welcomed in to the Kingdom and some won't, and faith is the determining factor.

The Sheep And Goat Judgment

Matt. 25:31 leaves no doubt as to its timing. It begins "When the Son of Man comes ... " and goes on to talk about the Lord setting up His throne on Earth after His return for the judgment of the nations, actually a judgment of Gentile tribulation survivors. The Lord doesn't judge nations in the eternal sense, only individuals. The Greek word here is ethnos, and means "people of every kind." They'll be judged by how they treated "His brothers" during the Great Tribulation. It's called the Sheep and Goat judgment, with the sheep being those who helped His brothers through the horrific times just past and goats being those who didn't.

Some say His brothers are believers, whether Jew or Gentile, and others say they're specifically Jews, but the most important point is that these tribulation survivors aren't being judged by their works. Their works are being cited as evidence of their faith, as in **James 2:18**. To give aid to a believer, especially a Jew, during the Great Tribulation will take even more courage than it did in Hitler's Germany, and according to some will be an offense punishable by death. Only a follower of Jesus, certain of His eternal destiny, would dare do it or even want to. Those who helped "His brothers" will have demonstrated their faith by their works and will be ushered live into the Kingdom. Those who refused to help will have condemned themselves to the outer darkness by this evidence of their lack of faith.

All three illustrations teach the same lesson. Surviving believers go live into the Kingdom. Some will have relied exclusively on the Holy Spirit's gift of faith, as in the Parable of the 10 Virgins. Others will have multiplied their faith by studying and sharing His word, as in the Parable of the Talents. Still others have put their faith into action, risking their lives in the bargain. They're the Sheep of the Sheep and Goat Judgment. But just like it's been throughout history, all are saved by faith.

Where's The Rapture?

The Sheep and Goat judgment is actually an expansion of **Matt. 24: 40-41** "One taken and the other left ... " Because of the timing problem, these verses can't be describing the Rapture. But there's more. The Greek word translated taken in verses 40 and 41 means "received." Captains choosing up sides in a sandlot baseball game point to someone and say, "I'll take you." It means, "Come over here. You're on my team." No problem so far, the Lord is taking some but not others.

But the primary meaning of the word translated left is "to send away" as a divorcing husband would "send away" his wife. In those days wives had no rights and except in very unusual circumstances didn't own property. The marriage home was the husband's property, usually built on his family's land. If he divorced his wife, he sent her away to live somewhere else, excluding her from his presence. Unbelievers won't be sent away in this manner at the Rapture. They'll be left in place to endure the judgments.

This passage isn't describing the Rapture. The timing, the context, and the disposition of the parties are all wrong. It's a summary of the Sheep and Goat judgment. Those taken (received) go live into the Kingdom in their natural bodies and help to re-populate the Earth, while those left (sent away) are put into the Outer Darkness, forever banned from the presence of God.

As it was in the days of Noah so shall it be at the coming of the Son of Man (**Matt. 24:37**) Let's back up now and address this overview statement. In the days of Noah the people of Earth could be separated into three groups. There were the unbelievers who perished in the Flood, Noah and his family, who were preserved through the Flood, and Enoch who was taken from Earth before the Flood. (Enoch was translated in **Genesis 5**. That means that God took him live into Heaven. The Flood came in **Genesis 6**.)

As the time of the End of the Age approaches the people of Earth will also fall into three groups. The unbelieving world will perish in the End Times judgments, Israel will be preserved through the judgments, and The Church will be taken from Earth before the judgments.

There are some interesting similarities between Enoch and the Church. His name means "teaching," one of the primary roles of the Church. Jewish tradition holds that Enoch was born on the 6th day of Sivan. The 6th of Sivan is the day in the Hebrew Calendar on which the Feast of Pentecost is celebrated. It's the day the Church was born. I think Enoch makes a good model of the Church. But you say, "Enoch was only one body." So is the Church.

At the 2nd Coming the door to salvation will be closed. The surviving people of Earth will be judged and those who've become believers will be welcomed into the Kingdom. Unbelievers will be taken off the planet, deprived of the Lord's presence forever. They wanted the Lord out of their lives, and now they'll get what they wanted.

6

The Duration and Purpose of the Millennium

Like rapture and Lucifer, millennium is a word of Latin origin and doesn't appear any where in the Scriptures. We get it from two Latin words, mille, or 1000, and annum, or year, from the Latin translation of **Rev. 20:6**. Mille annum, millennium, the Lord's 1000-year reign on Earth, is known to Israel as the Kingdom Age. It's the seventh and final thousand years of the Age of Man, begun with the birth of Adam. It's often confused with Eternity, but as we saw earlier the two are distinct. A Millennium is obviously a defined span of time, while by definition Eternity is the absence of time as we know it.

The Millennium On Earth

During the Millennium, the Lord will be King of Heaven and Earth, Earth being restored to the condition it was in when Adam was created. This will include restoring peace between man and the animals, bringing back Earth's original garden-like environment with its world wide sub-tropical climate, eliminating foul weather, killer storms, earthquakes and extremes of heat and cold.

The span of man's life will begin increasing again to equal those of the Genesis patriarchs. Sickness and disease, those by-products of sin, will be greatly reduced. It appears the population of Earth will be sustained by the return to an agrarian economy, but with all the obstacles Adam faced gone as the curse of **Genesis 3** is finally lifted. Man will easily produce enough for his family's use, and enjoy doing it. None will labor unproductively, or primarily for the benefit of others. Children will grow up without fear and adults will grow old in peace. (All the above is a summary of **Isaiah 2:1-5, 4:2-6, 35, 41:18-20, 60:10-22, 65:17-25, Micah 4:1-8**)

Since Earth will be re-populated mostly by Tribulation survivors in their natural bodies, there will still be sin although to a much lesser extent, especially at the beginning. In the so-called Millennial Temple in Israel, priests will conduct daily sacrifices for sin, just like in Old Testament days. But while Old Testament believers observed Temple sacrifices to learn what the Messiah would one day do for them, Millennial believers will observe them to remember, and their children to learn, what He's already done. (**Ezek 40-47**)

The Lord will reign supreme on Earth as King and High Priest, the head of both a one-world government and a one-world religion. He'll brook no threats to His established peace, nor any deviation from His doctrine. (**Psalm 2**)

At the beginning, only believers will inhabit Earth, enjoying the truly utopian environment that mankind has always dreamed about, but only God can create. They'll soon begin bearing children who, as they mature, will have to choose to receive the Lord's pardon just as we have. And as it is today some will reject Him to go their own way. By the time Satan is released at the end of the Millennium, there will be so many who've rejected the Lord that he'll quickly find a huge army of recruits for his final attempt to kick the Lord off the planet.

But with fire from Heaven the Lord will destroy Satan's army, casting him into the Lake of Fire, where he'll be tormented day and night forever. Never again will he or any of his accomplices be free to afflict God's people. (**Rev. 20:7-10**)

How Did That Happen?

What began as an age of unimagined peace and prosperity will have ended in open warfare against the very King who made it possible. How could this be?

Before the Millennium, man had three excuses for his inability to please God. The first was Satan, whose clever schemes led man astray. But all during the Millennium, Satan will be bound in darkness.

The second was the bad influence of unbelievers. But as the Millennium begins, Earth will have been cleansed of all its unbelievers. Only those who had given their hearts to the Lord will be allowed to enter the Kingdom.

And the third was God's absence from our midst. For 2600 years, with the exception of one 33 year period, God will have been absent from the planet leaving man to "fend for himself." But all during the Millennium Father, Son, and Holy Spirit will have dwelt in the midst of the people of Earth.

What's The Point?

In the Millennium, Earth dwellers will live in the ideal circumstances that Adam and Eve enjoyed in the Garden of Eden. The curse will be gone and the Lord will be there among them, everyone's a believer and Satan will be bound. And yet, there's enough residual sin in the hearts of unregenerate man that he'll rebel the first chance he gets. Sinful man cannot dwell in the presence of a Holy God, being unable to keep His commandments. He needs a Savior and Redeemer to reconcile him to God, and a heart transplant to cure him of his sin nature.

The whole point of the Millennium is to prove once and for all that man's heart is deceitful above all things and beyond cure (**Jere. 17:9**) making it impossible for him to live in a manner pleasing to God.

The Millennium In the New Jerusalem

Life is far different in the Home of the Redeemed Church. Although the Kings of the Earth bring us their splendor, no unbeliever can ever set foot in the place, nor even a believer in his natural state. Our mansions in the sky are built of the purest gold as are the streets that run before them, their foundations made from precious stones. There's no Temple in the New Jerusalem because the Lamb of God dwells there and is our Temple. The energy source that lights and warms us is the Glory of God, and our radiance in turn provides light for the nations of Earth. (**Rev.21:9-27**)

Our glorified bodies will have been released from their dimensional bonds, allowing us to appear and disappear at will, traveling back and forth through time at the speed of thought as we plumb the limitless delights of God's Creation. No detail has been overlooked where our comfort and happiness are concerned. There's no more death or mourning or crying or pain, only the endless joys of exploration and discovery. *As it is written: "No eye has seen, no ear has heard, no mind has conceived what God has prepared for those who love him."* (**1 Cor. 2:9**)

Our home is not on Earth, but it's not at the Throne of God either. Coming down out of the heavens but never landing on Earth, our home could be called a low orbit satellite in today's terminology. 1400 miles high, wide and deep, it wouldn't fit in Israel, let alone Jerusalem. If we did touch down on Earth we'd need a space equivalent to the area from Maine to Florida to the Midwest, or all of Western Europe from Sweden to Italy, and the New Jerusalem will be over 4000 times as tall as the world's tallest building. Nearly 2/3rds the size of the Moon, it simply won't fit anywhere on Earth.

The Church has been described as the Pearl of Great Price. A pearl is created in the ocean and grows as a response to an irritant. It's the only precious gem to come from a living organism. At harvest time, it's removed from its natural habitat to be placed in a custom made setting where it becomes an object of adornment.

And so it is with the Church. Created from among the Gentile nations, the Church was a major irritant to both Israel and the Roman Empire. Though hundreds of years of persecution were intended for our destruction, we grew steadily. At the harvest we'll be taken from Earth to be placed in mansions the Lord has built especially for us, to become the object of His adornment.

7

Eternity

I can't say much about eternity except to tell you that there is one. The Bible ends at the end of the Millennium, yet teaches us that every one ever born lives forever. The question is not whether you have eternal life. The question is where you will spend eternity. There are only two possible destinations and we've described them both. Eternal bliss in the presence of God, or eternal shame and punishment banished from the presence of God. While God is patient, not desiring that any should be lost, it's not His decision to make. He's given it to you, knowing that without an alternative, your choice to accept Him would be meaningless. He loves you enough to risk that you'll make the wrong decision, and enough to abide by your wishes if you do.

Don't get me wrong. No one would knowingly choose to go to a place of eternal torment. But many will wind up there. When they do it'll be because they refused to choose Heaven, and it's the only other alternative.

Here then are Seven Things you Have To Know To Understand End Times Prophecy. Mastering them will allow you to successfully avoid all the heresy and false teaching that swirls about in these last days. The study of prophecy is not a salvation issue, but the Lord did admonish us on several occasions to understand the signs of the times so we wouldn't be caught off guard. We are to watch with expectation and wait with certainty.

In **Revelation 1:3** we're promised blessings for our diligent study, and in **2 Timothy 4:8** a crown for longing for His appearing. But to me the greatest gift that comes from studying prophecy is the strengthening of our faith. Nothing can equal watching the Word of God proceed from abstract to concrete as we see Bible Prophecy fulfilled before our very eyes. If you listen carefully, you can almost hear the Footsteps of the Messiah.

Appendices

1. The 70 Weeks Of Daniel
2. The Battle Of Ezekiel 38-39
3. Psalm 83
4. Isaiah 17, An Oracle Against Damascus
5. The Olivet Discourse
6. Defending The Pre-Tribulation Rapture Of The Church
7. The Coming Temple

Appendix 1

The Seventy Weeks of Daniel

Many believe that **Daniel 9:24-27** is the most important passage of prophecy in all of Scripture. Almost every mistake I've run across in studying the various interpretations of End Times Prophecy can be traced back to a misunderstanding of this passage. Let's undertake a study of this important prophecy.

Before plowing into it we'll back up a little and review the context. Daniel was an old man, probably in his eighties. He'd been in Babylon for nearly 70 years and knew from reading the scroll of Jeremiah's writings (specifically the part we know as **Jeremiah 25:8-11**) that the 70-year captivity God had ordained for Israel was just about over (**Daniel 9:2**).

The reason for the captivity had been Israel's insistence upon worshiping the false gods of their pagan neighbors. Its duration of 70 years came from the fact that for 490 years they had failed to let their farmland lie fallow one year out of every seven as God had commanded in **Leviticus 25:1-7**. The Lord had been patient all that time but finally had sent them to Babylon to give the land the 70 years of rest that were due it. (**2 Chron. 36:21**)

The beginning of **Daniel 9** documents Daniel's prayer, reminding the Lord that the 70 year time of punishment was nearly over and asking for mercy on behalf of his people. Before he could finish his prayer, the angel Gabriel appeared to him and spoke the words that we know as **Daniel 9:24-27**. Let's read the whole thing to get the overview and then take it apart verse by verse.

Seventy weeks are determined upon your people and your Holy City to finish transgression, to put an end to sin, to atone for wickedness, to bring in everlasting righteousness, to seal up vision and prophecy and to anoint the most Holy. Know and understand this: From the issuing of the decree to restore and rebuild Jerusalem until The Anointed One the Ruler comes there will be seven weeks and sixty two weeks. It will be rebuilt with streets and a trench but in times of trouble. After the sixty two weeks the Anointed One will be cut off and have nothing. The people of the ruler who will come will destroy the city and the sanctuary. The end will come like a flood: War will continue till the end and desolations have been decreed. He will confirm a covenant with many for one week. In the middle of the week he will put an end to sacrifice and offering. And on a wing of the Temple he will set up an abomination that causes desolation until the end that is decreed is poured out on him (**Daniel 9:24-27**).

No prophecy in all of Scripture is more critical to our understanding of the end times than these four verses. A few basic clarifications are in order first, then we'll interpret the passage verse by verse. The Hebrew word translated weeks (or sevens) refers to a period of 7 years, like the English word decade refers to a period of 10 years. It literally means "a week of years." So 70 weeks is 70 X 7 years or 490 years. This period is divided into three parts, 7 weeks or 49 years, 62 weeks or 434 years, and 1 week or 7 years. Let's begin.

Seventy weeks are determined upon your people and your Holy City to finish transgression, to put an end to sin, to atone for wickedness, to bring in everlasting righteousness, to seal up vision and prophecy and to anoint the most Holy (place) (**Daniel 9:24**).

Sitting upon His heavenly throne, God decreed that six things would be accomplished for Daniel's people (Israel) and Daniel's Holy City (Jerusalem) during a specified period of 490 years. (I've inserted the word "place" after Holy at the end of the verse to clarify the fact that it refers to the Jewish Temple in Jerusalem.)

We should be aware that in Hebrew these things read a little differently. Literally, God had determined to;

1. restrict or restrain the transgression (also translated rebellion)
2. seal up their sins (as if putting them away in a sealed container)
3. make atonement (restitution) for their iniquity
4. bring them into a state of everlasting righteousness
5. seal up (same word as #2) vision and prophecy
6. anoint (consecrate) the most Holy place (sanctuary)

In plain language, God would put an end to their rebellion against Him, put away their sins and pay the penalties they had accrued, bring the people into a state of perpetual righteousness, fulfill the remaining prophecies, and anoint the Temple.

This was to be accomplished through their Messiah (Jesus) because no one else could do it. Had they accepted Him as their savior their rebellion against God would have ended. Their sins would have all been forgiven, and the full penalty paid for them. They would have entered into a state of eternal righteousness, all their prophecies would have been fulfilled and the rebuilt temple would have been consecrated. It should be noted here that although it appears to have been accepted by Him, God never dwelt in the 2nd Temple, nor was the ark of the covenant and its mercy seat ever present therein.

Know and understand this: From the issuing of the decree to restore and rebuild Jerusalem until The Anointed One the Ruler comes there will be seven weeks and sixty two weeks. It will be rebuilt with streets and a trench but in times of trouble (**Daniel 9:25**).

Here is a clear prophecy of the timing of the First Coming. When this message was given to Daniel by the angel Gabriel, Jerusalem had lain in ruin for nearly 70 years and the Jews were captive in Babylon. Counting forward for 62 + 7 periods of 7 years each (a total of 483 years) from a future decree giving the Jews permission to restore and rebuild Jerusalem, they should expect the Messiah.

To avoid confusion, it's important to distinguish the decree that freed the Jews from their captivity from the one that gave them permission to rebuild Jerusalem.

When he conquered Babylon in 535BC Cyrus the Persian immediately freed the Jews. It had been prophesied 150 years earlier in **Isaiah 44:24-45:6** and was fulfilled in **Ezra 1:1-4**. But according to **Nehemiah 2:1** the decree to rebuild Jerusalem was given in the first month of the 20th year of his reign by King Artaxerxes of Persia (March of 445 BC on our calendar, about 90 years later).

Exactly 483 years after that decree the Lord Jesus rode in to Jerusalem on a donkey to shouts of "Hosanna"! It was the only day in His life that He permitted His followers to proclaim Him as Israel's King, fulfilling Daniel's prophecy to the day! The Hebrew in **Daniel 9:25** calls Him Messiah the Prince, denoting the fact that He was coming as the Anointed Son of the King and was not yet crowned King Himself.

In **Luke 19:41-45**, Jesus reminded the people of the specific nature of this prophecy. As he approached Jerusalem and saw the city, he wept over it and said,

"If you, even you, had only known on this day what would bring you peace—but now it is hidden from your eyes. The days will come upon you when your enemies will build an embankment against you and encircle you and hem you in on every side. They will dash you to the ground, you and the children within your walls. They will not leave one stone on another, because you did not recognize the time of God's coming to you."

He held them accountable for knowing **Daniel 9:24-27**.

A few days later He extended that accountability to those who would be alive in Israel during the End Times.

"So when you see standing in the holy place 'the abomination that causes desolation,' spoken of through the prophet Daniel—let the reader understand— then let those who are in Judea flee to the mountains. (**Matt 24:15-16**)

They will also be required to understand **Daniel 9**.

After the sixty two weeks the Anointed One will be cut off and have nothing. The people of the ruler who will come will destroy the city and the sanctuary.

The end will come like a flood: War will continue till the end and desolations have been decreed (**Daniel 9:26**).

First came 7 sevens (49 years) and then 62 sevens (434 years) for a total of 69 sevens or 483 years. The Hebrew word for Anointed One is Mashaich (Messiah in English). At the end of this 2nd period their Messiah would be cut off, which means to be executed or literally destroyed in the making of a covenant, having received none of the honor, glory and blessing the Scriptures promised Him.

Make no mistake about it. Jesus had to die so these 6 promises could come true. No one else in Heaven or on Earth could accomplish this. We can only imagine how different things would have been if they had accepted Him as their Messiah and let Him die for their sins so He could bring them into everlasting righteousness with His resurrection. But of course God knew they wouldn't, so He had to do things the hard way.

Do you realize what that means? It wasn't killing the Messiah that put the Jews at odds with God. After all He came to die for them. No. It's that in killing Him, they refused to let His death pay for their sins so He could save them. This had the effect of making His death meaningless to them. That's what severed the relationship.

Because of that, we now get the first hint that all would not go well. Following the crucifixion the people of a ruler yet to come would destroy Jerusalem and the Temple, the same Temple that God decreed would be consecrated. The Israelites would be scattered abroad and peace would elude the world.

We all know that Jesus was crucified and 38 years later the Romans put the torch to the city and the Temple destroying both. Surviving Jews were forced to flee for their lives and in the ensuing 2000 years I don't believe a single generation has escaped involvement in a war of some kind.

After the crucifixion something strange happened: The Heavenly clock stopped. 69 of the 70 weeks had passed and all that was prophesied to happen during those 483 years had come to pass but there was still one week (7 years) left. There are hints in the Old Testament that the clock had stopped several times before in Israel's history when for one reason or another they were either under subjugation or out of the land. And in the New Testament we're also given hints that while God is dealing with the Church, time ceases to exist for Israel (**Acts 15:13-18**). But the clearest indication of the stopped clock is that the events foretold in **Daniel 9:27** simply haven't happened yet.

He will confirm a covenant with many for one week. In the middle of the week he will put an end to sacrifice and offering. And on a wing of the Temple he will set up an abomination that causes desolation until the end that is decreed is poured out on him (**Daniel 9:27**).

It's vital to our understanding of the End Times that we realize two things here. First, the Age of

Grace (Church Age) didn't follow the Age of Law, it merely interrupted the Age of Law seven years short of its promised duration. These seven years have to be completed for God to accomplish the six things the angel listed in verse 24 for Israel.

And second, the Age of Grace was not the next step in the progression of God's overall plan, but was a deviation from it. Once the rapture comes, nothing like the Age of Grace will ever happen again (**Ephes. 2:6-7**). Even when Israel accepts the New Covenant, as **Jeremiah 31:31-34** promises, they won't enjoy the same benefits the Church has enjoyed. The relationship the Church has with the Lord will never be repeated with any other group. Ever.

But before we try to understand the 70th week let's review a rule of grammar that will help make our interpretation correct. The rule is this: Pronouns refer us back to the closest previous noun. "He", being a personal pronoun, refers to the closest previous personal noun, in this case the "ruler who will come." So a ruler who will come from the territory of the old Roman Empire will confirm a 7 year covenant with Israel that permits them to build a Temple and re-instate their Old Covenant worship system. 3 1/2 years later he will violate the covenant by setting up an abomination that causes the Temple to become desolate, putting an end to their worship. This abomination brings the wrath of God down upon him and he will be destroyed.

The most obvious way in which we know these things haven't happened is that the Jewish Old Covenant worship system requires a Temple and there hasn't been one since 70 AD when the Romans destroyed it.

Some say this prophecy was fulfilled during the Roman destruction but most believe it's yet future, partly because of the term Abomination that causes Desolation. It's a specific insult to God that has happened only once previously. Antiochus Epiphanes, a powerful Syrian king, had attacked Jerusalem and entered the Temple area in 168BC. There he had sacrificed a pig on the Temple altar and erected a statue of the Greek god Zeus with his own face on it. He then required everyone to worship it on pain of death. This rendered the Temple unfit for worshiping God and so incensed the Jews that they revolted and defeated the Syrians. This is all recorded in Jewish history (1st Maccabees) where it's called the Abomination of Desolation. The subsequent cleansing of the Temple is celebrated to this day in the Feast of Hanukkah.

Paul warned us that in the latter days a world leader will become so powerful that he will exalt himself above everything that is called god or is worshiped and will stand in the Temple proclaiming himself to be God (**2 Thes 2:4**). In **Rev 13:14-15** we're told that he'll have a statue of himself erected and require everyone to worship it on pain of death. In **Matt 24:15-21** Jesus said that the Abomination that causes Desolation spoken of by Daniel will kick off the Great Tribulation, a period of time 3 1/2 years long that coincides with the last half of Daniel's 70th week. The similarities between this coming event and the one from history being so obvious, most scholars are persuaded that one points to the other since nothing in the intervening years fits so completely.

Soon And Very Soon

A new leader will soon emerge on the scene, a man with great personal charisma. Following a devastating war in the Middle East he'll present a plan to restore peace, by which he will quickly captivate and control the world (**Daniel 8:23-25**). Since all true believers will have recently disappeared from Earth in the rapture of the Church, he'll have no trouble persuading most remaining inhabitants that he is the promised Messiah, the Prince of Peace. He will astound and amaze them all with feats of diplomacy and conquest, even performing the supernatural.

When he claims to be God, all hell will break loose on Earth and 3 1/2 years of the most terrible times mankind has ever known will threaten their very existence. But before they're all destroyed the real Prince of Peace will return and overthrow this impostor. He will set up His kingdom on earth, a kingdom that will never be destroyed or left to another.

Having given His life to finish transgression, put an end to sin, atone for wickedness and bring in everlasting righteousness, and having fulfilled all Biblical vision and prophecy, He will anoint the most Holy Place and receive all the honor, glory and blessing the Scriptures promise Him. Israel will finally have her Kingdom back and will live in peace with God in her midst forever. You can almost hear the footsteps of the Messiah.

Appendix 2

The Battle Of Ezekiel 38-39

I first began studying **Ezekiel 38** in the 1980's and have watched with great interest as our changing world conforms more and more to Ezekiel's words. As the time of the end draws nearer the insights we gain from the changes around us give us a better understanding of Bible prophecy in general and **Ezekiel 38** in particular. In this update of our study we'll apply these insights to Ezekiel's 2600 year old prophecy.

What Time Is It?

First of all, let's get some kind of time frame settled. Ezekiel's prophecies are chronological. Falling between the prophecies of Israel's modern re-birth (**Ezekiel 36-37**) and the Millennium (**Ezekiel 40-48**), the battle of **Ezekiel 38-39** has to take place during a time of peace after 1948 but before the 2nd coming, and all agree it hasn't happened yet. This has led some to see the passage as a description of Armageddon, but as we'll see there are many prominent nations missing from this battle whereas **Zechariah 14:2** prophecies that every nation will join the battle of Armageddon. That being the case, the time frame narrows to sometime between 1948 and the beginning of the Great Tribulation, after which no place in the world will be at peace, especially Israel.

Ezekiel prophesied that the Lord would use this battle to turn Israel back to Him and to complete the return of Jews from all over the world to Israel, not leaving any behind (**Ezekiel 39:28**). This leads us to believe that the battle of **Ezekiel 38-39** is the event that re-starts the clock on the 490-year period of time spoken of by Daniel, the famous 70 weeks of **Daniel 9:24-27**. 69 of those weeks (483 years) had come when the Messiah was crucified and the Temple destroyed, stopping the clock one week (seven years) short of fulfillment. I believe the dramatic victory the Lord wins over Israel's enemies in Ezekiel's battle will convince them to officially re-instate their Old Covenant relationship with Him to fulfill the remaining seven years of Daniel's prophecy.

This will require two things to happen. First they'll need a Temple for worship. It's this Temple that's later desecrated by the anti-Christ, kicking off the Great Tribulation. And second, the Church will have to disappear. Paul wrote that Israel had been hardened in part until the full number of Gentiles has come in (**Romans 11:25**). That means as long as the Church is around Israel won't be able to recognize God's involvement in their national life.

But the Battle of Ezekiel 38 will be such a miraculous victory that it will re-awaken Israel to God's presence. This means the Age of Grace will have come to an end and the Church will be gone by the time this battle comes to an end.

With all this in mind, let's begin a careful study of **Ezekiel 38-39**, to prepare us for these long prophesied events that will become reality soon.

The word of the LORD came to me: "Son of man, set your face against Gog, of the land of Magog, the chief prince of Meshech and Tubal; prophesy against him and say: 'This is what the Sovereign LORD says: I am against you, O Gog, chief prince of Meshech and Tubal. I will turn you around, put hooks in your jaws and bring you out with your whole army-your horses, your horsemen fully armed, and a great horde with large and small shields, all of them brandishing their swords. Persia, Cush and Put will be with them, all with shields and helmets, also Gomer with all its troops and Beth Togarmah from the far north with all its troops-the many nations with you. (**Ezek. 38:1-6**)

I believe that Gog is a supernatural figure (perhaps Satan's counterpart to the Archangel Michael) and the behind the scenes commander of this event, while Magog is listed in **Genesis 10** as one of Noah's grandsons, a son of Japeth. Over 130 historical references demonstrate that Magog is the father of today's Russian people.

The phrase "hooks in the jaw" comes from the equestrian world where a special bridle is used to make a rebellious horse obedient to its rider's commands. It symbolizes God forcing Russia to become involved in this battle to assure that His will is done.

Persia is the ancient name for Iran, Cush and Put represent the North African nations, Gomer was Magog's brother and settled along the Danube River in what would become Eastern Europe, and Togarmah, a son of Gomer, inhabited what's now known as Turkey. The characteristic all these nations have in common today is their religion. They're all Moslem.

"Get ready; be prepared, you and all the hordes gathered about you, and take command of them. After many days you will be called to arms. In future years you will invade a land that has recovered from war, whose people were gathered from many nations to the mountains of Israel, which had long been desolate. They had been brought out from the nations, and now all of them live in safety. You and all your troops and the many nations with you will go up, advancing like a storm; you will be like a cloud covering the land. (**Ezek. 38:7-9**)

The fact that Israel is the target in this passage is self evident, but a controversy rages around the Heberew word betach translated "in safety" in verse 8. A secondary meaning, "carelessly" could mean that they're not really safe but just think they are and so their guard is down. To achieve either of the conditions this word implies would require a truly miraculous change in Israel's current situation and for many years scholars were uncertain as to how this could ever happen.

But a little known prophecy in the Psalms might have the answer. According to **Psalm 83** all of Israel's next door neighbors will unite in an effort to wipe Israel completely off the map. But Israel will soundly defeat them and capture their lands as well. Enemies like Hezbollah, Lebanon, the Palestinians, Hamas, etc. will cease to exist, and the lands they now occupy will once again belong to Israel. (Many people don't realize that even the land of Lebanon was originally given to Israel and will belong to Israel again in the Millennium.)

It's also beginning to look like the **Isaiah 17** prophecy of the destruction of Damascus could be fulfilled at the same time. Israel has officially declared that they'll hold Syria responsible for any attack by Hezbollah, and will retaliate accordingly. High Israeli officials have recently said that the Syrian government will not survive such a retaliation and its infrastructure will be destroyed. This is a direct threat against Damascus. (You can read more about **Psalm 83** and **Isaiah 17** in appendices 3 and 4.)

If the fulfillment of **Psalm 83** and **Isaiah 17** precede the Battle **Ezekiel 38**, it helps explain how Israel could be taken by surprise when the Moslem coalition attacks and why none of Israel's next door neighbors are mentioned in Ezekiel's line up.

Conditions are quickly falling into place for the fulfillment of **Ezekiel 38-39**. Turkey has all but declared itself part of the Moslem coalition after years of being one of Israel's most reliable allies. As for Israel's great protector the USA, our current leaders have withdrawn their support to a point where no one can say for sure how we would respond in case of an attack on Israel. Jewish officials suspect our recent pledges of support are just empty words, meant only for public consumption.

If so, all that remains for **Ezekiel 38** to happen is for Israel to become confident enough in their military prowess to believe no one would attack them. The fulfillment of prophecies in **Psalm 83** and **Isaiah 17** could prompt such a careless state of mind, and some informed sources are predicting that these battles could take place as early as this year. Time will tell.

But in the meantime, to freshen our prophetic perspective, we'll continue our review of **Ezekiel 38-39**.

"This is what the Sovereign LORD says: On that day thoughts will come into your mind and you will devise an evil scheme. You will say, "I will invade a land of unwalled villages; I will attack a peaceful and unsuspecting people-all of them living without walls and without gates and bars. I will plunder and loot and turn my hand against the resettled ruins and the people gathered from the nations, rich in livestock and goods, living at the center of the land." Sheba and Dedan and the merchants of Tarshish and all her villages will say to you, "Have you come to plunder? Have you gathered your hordes to loot, to carry off

silver and gold, to take away livestock and goods and to seize much plunder?" ' **(Ezek. 38:10-13)**

Israel is described here as a country at peace in the idiom of Ezekiel's day, a land of unwalled villages. In Biblical times villages only built protective walls if they were concerned about being attacked. Israel won't be expecting war. When this enemy coalition suddenly and unexpectedly attacks, other countries not involved will take notice. They won't know what's going on either.

Sheba and Dedan are first mentioned as grandsons of Cush in **Genesis 10:7**. Later, in **Genesis 25:3**, we read of grandsons of Abraham named Sheba and Dedan as well, born to Jokshan, a son of Abraham and his 2nd wife, Keturah.

From the passage it's not clear which pair of grandsons is being referenced, but commentaries none-the-less identify these two as representing the nations of the Arabian Peninsula, notably Saudi Arabia. According to archaeologists W. F. Albright and Wendell Phillips, Sheba was on the south-western edge of the Arabian Peninsula across the Red Sea from present-day Ethiopia. Sheba is known in history as Saba in Southern Arabia, home to the Sabaeans of classical geography, who carried on the trade in spices with the other peoples of the ancient world. Dedan was probably the habitat of the Arabs in the northern part of the Arabian Desert, which is modern-day Saudi Arabia. The ancient capital of Saudi Arabia is still called Dedan on many maps today.

Tarshish was a son of Javan, who settled the area of southern Greece. Some see his name as a reference to ancient Tartessus, a seaport in southern Spain, near Gibraltar. Others recall the sea going navies of the Phoenicians who sailed "the Ships of Tarshish" out of nearby Cadiz as far north as England for tin, a metal used in the making of bronze and other alloys, which they mined in Cornwall.

Some believe that the name Britannia is actually derived from a Phoenician word meaning "source of tin." If so, since the ships of Tarshish brought tin to the ancient world, this reference could be to Great Britain making the "lions" (KJV) or "villages"(NIV) of Tarshish Great Britain's colonies, of which the US is the most prominent today. The fact that the Lion is a symbol of the British Empire lends support to this view.

This is the main reason I don't believe this battle is the Armageddon of **Revelation 16:16**. There are too many significant countries that aren't involved, when according to **Zechariah 14:2** all the nations of the world will be gathered against Jerusalem for the final battle.

"Therefore, son of man, prophesy and say to Gog: 'This is what the Sovereign LORD says: In that day, when my people Israel are living in safety, will you not take notice of it? You will come from your place in the far north, you and many nations with you, all of them riding on horses, a great horde, a mighty army. You will advance against my people Israel like a cloud that covers the land. In days to come, O Gog,

I will bring you against my land, so that the nations may know me when I show myself holy through you before their eyes. (**Ezek. 38:14-16**)

Here the Lord makes His intent unmistakably clear. He's orchestrating this event to reveal Himself to the world once again. The years and years of debate over God's existence, begun with the German School of Higher Criticism in the 1800's and continued in the modern rationalism of the 1950's will be put to naught as God uses this battle to poke His head through the fabric of the sky and shout, "I'm still here!"

"'This is what the Sovereign LORD says: Are you not the one I spoke of in former days by my servants the prophets of Israel? At that time they prophesied for years that I would bring you against them. This is what will happen in that day: When Gog attacks the land of Israel, my hot anger will be aroused, declares the Sovereign LORD. In my zeal and fiery wrath I declare that at that time there shall be a great earthquake in the land of Israel.

The fish of the sea, the birds of the air, the beasts of the field, every creature that moves along the ground, and all the people on the face of the earth will tremble at my presence. The mountains will be overturned, the cliffs will crumble and every wall will fall to the ground. I will summon a sword against Gog on all my mountains, declares the Sovereign LORD. Every man's sword will be against his brother. I will exe-

cute judgment upon him with plague and bloodshed; I will pour down torrents of rain, hailstones and burning sulfur on him and on his troops and on the many nations with him. And so I will show my greatness and my holiness, and I will make myself known in the sight of many nations. Then they will know that I am the LORD.' (**Ezek. 38:17-23**)

When the Moslem coalition attacks Israel, God will say, *"You're the ones I had Ezekiel warn my people about so long ago."* With signs reminiscent of all the Heaven-fought wars of the past, the Lord is aroused in anger to execute judgment against the invaders of His land and enemies of His people.

And as He has done before, He will sew confusion in the hearts of Israel's enemies so that they commence attacking themselves while He unleashes the classic weapons of divine retribution. Earthquakes, plagues, bloodshed, rain, hailstones, and burning sulfur; these are His signature signs. Neither Israel, nor the enemy coalition, nor those watching from afar will fail to interpret them correctly.

Ezekiel 39

"Son of man, prophesy against Gog and say: 'This is what the Sovereign LORD says: I am against you, O Gog, chief prince of Meshech and Tubal. I will turn you around and drag you along. I will bring you from the far north and send you against the mountains of Israel. Then I will strike your bow from your left hand and make your arrows drop from your right hand. On the mountains of Israel you will fall, you

and all your troops and the nations with you. I will give you as food to all kinds of carrion birds and to the wild animals. You will fall in the open field, for I have spoken, declares the Sovereign LORD. I will send fire on Magog and on those who live in safety in the coastlands, and they will know that I am the LORD.

"'I will make known my holy name among my people Israel. I will no longer let my holy name be profaned, and the nations will know that I the LORD am the Holy One in Israel. It is coming! It will surely take place, declares the Sovereign LORD. This is the day I have spoken of. (**Ezek. 39:1-8**)

The King James has the more accurate rendering for the beginning of this passage. The phrase translated I will turn you around and drag you along in the NIV and others, literally reads I will turn you around and leave but the sixth part of you, which means that 5/6ths of the Moslem armies will be destroyed.

The Hebrew concept is roughly equivalent to the one behind the English word "decimate." Although decimate originally described the punishment requiring that 1 in 10 soldiers in a mutinous Roman Legion be executed, figuratively it has come to mean that something is all but totally destroyed. Synonyms are "annihilate" or "wipe out." So it is with the Hebrew. When the Lord brings this Moslem coalition into the mountains of Israel, He will also wipe them out.

And don't be confused by the reference to bows and arrows. Ezekiel was just using terms he knew. The same Hebrew words could be translated launchers and missiles today.

Some interpret the idea of sending fire on Magog and those who live safely in the coast lands as warning of a nuclear exchange. Magog refers to Russia of course, but the identity of the coast lands is less clear. The Hebrew word implies that they're a distant land, and in Isaiah the phrase "beyond the sea" is used to help locate them, the sea being the Mediterranean. This reference could easily be pointing to Europe, and some even believe the US is in focus here. But we'll have to wait and see.

Also the Hebrew word translated in safety is the same one that's used to describe Israel's state of mind in **Ezek. 38:8**. Again it denotes a sense of care-lessness, this time on Europe's part, as if they don't believe this kind of thing could happen to them and therefore aren't prepared for what's coming.

And once more the Lord explains His real purpose. He's going to use this battle to announce to one and all that He's Israel's Protector and Champion. The nations of the world are being told that to get to Israel, they'll have to go through Him.

"'Then those who live in the towns of Israel will go out and use the weapons for fuel and burn them up-the small and large shields, the bows and arrows, the war clubs and spears. For seven years they will use them for fuel. They will not need to gather wood from the fields or cut it from the forests, because they

will use the weapons for fuel. And they will plunder those who plundered them and loot those who looted them, declares the Sovereign LORD. (**Ezek 39:9-10**)

In Ezekiel's day people burned wood for heat and so that's the idiom he used to describe the situation. In fact, the passage indicates that all of Israel's energy needs for 7 years will be met by converting the energy from the weapons the enemy leaves behind to peaceful use. I can't imagine the enemy carrying in enough wood (or any other conventional fuel for that matter) to supply Israel's power and heating plants for 7 years, so a more modern application is in order.

Many observers say this is a reference to nuclear power. The old Soviet Union converted submarine reactors into power generating plants to provide electricity for whole communities so the notion isn't that far fetched. And as you'll see, the clean-up procedures for this battle are remarkably similar to today's nuclear decontamination process.

Why only 7 years then, when a nuclear reactor could theoretically supply energy needs for much longer? If, as I believe, this battle will introduce the 70th week of Daniel, 7 years worth of energy is all they'll need. After that, the Lord will supply their needs. (**Rev. 22:5**)

"'On that day I will give Gog a burial place in Israel, in the valley of those who travel east toward the Sea. It will block the way of travelers, because Gog and all his hordes will be buried there. So it will be called the Valley of Hamon Gog.

"'For seven months the house of Israel will be burying them in order to cleanse the land. All the people of the land will bury them, and the day I am glorified will be a memorable day for them, declares the Sovereign LORD.

"'Men will be regularly employed to cleanse the land. Some will go throughout the land and, in addition to them, others will bury those that remain on the ground. At the end of the seven months they will begin their search. As they go through the land and one of them sees a human bone, he will set up a marker beside it until the gravediggers have buried it in the Valley of Hamon Gog. (Also a town called Hamonah will be there.) And so they will cleanse the land' **(Ezek 39:11-16)**

The King James version says this valley is east of the Dead Sea. If so it would be in Jordan, not Israel, and even in Ezekiel's day would have been outside Israel's borders. Yet verse 11 clearly locates the burial place in Israel. Therefore I believe it's more likely the one traditionally called the Valley of the Shadow of Death **(Psalm 23:4)** that was part of Israel during Ezekiel's time. If so, it's at the bottom of the old Jericho Road that still connects Jerusalem with Jericho and is on the way to the Dead Sea. And remarkably it's in territory occupied by the Palestinians today, another hint that due to the fulfillment of **Psalm 83** they will have lost any claim to the West Bank before Ezekiel's Battle begins.

It will require the combined efforts of all Israeli citizens for 7 months to bury the enemy dead. After that they'll hire professionals, some to decontaminate the land and some to search for any bodies the people may have missed. They won't touch any bones they find, but will set up markers and call the professionals to come take them away. This approach fits modern Nuclear Biological Chemical Warfare decontamination procedures to a tee. Did the Lord have Ezekiel write this to show us the type of weaponry being used? Between this and the energy reference above, it sure looks that way.

"Son of man, this is what the Sovereign LORD says: Call out to every kind of bird and all the wild animals: 'Assemble and come together from all around to the sacrifice I am preparing for you, the great sacrifice on the mountains of Israel. There you will eat flesh and drink blood. You will eat the flesh of mighty men and drink the blood of the princes of the earth as if they were rams and lambs, goats and bulls-all of them fattened animals from Bashan. At the sacrifice I am preparing for you, you will eat fat till you are glutted and drink blood till you are drunk. At my table you will eat your fill of horses and riders, mighty men and soldiers of every kind,' declares the Sovereign LORD. (**Ezek. 39:17-20**)

The carrion birds and scavengers will have a field day due to the carnage left behind on the battlefield. Earlier the enemy force was described as being a great horde, like a cloud covering the land. Now that it's been decimated there are dead bodies everywhere. This is not unique in Israel's history. Josephus wrote that after the Battle of the Galilee in 68 AD there were so many dead bodies floating in the Sea that you couldn't see the water.

"I will display my glory among the nations, and all the nations will see the punishment I inflict and the hand I lay upon them. From that day forward the house of Israel will know that I am the LORD their God. And the nations will know that the people of Israel went into exile for their sin, because they were unfaithful to me. So I hid my face from them and handed them over to their enemies, and they all fell by the sword. I dealt with them according to their uncleanness and their offenses, and I hid my face from them.

"Therefore this is what the Sovereign LORD says: I will now bring Jacob back from captivity and will have compassion on all the people of Israel, and I will be zealous for my holy name. They will forget their shame and all the unfaithfulness they showed toward me when they lived in safety in their land with no one to make them afraid. When I have brought them back from the nations and have gathered them from the countries of their enemies, I will show myself holy through them in the sight of many nations. Then they will know that I am the LORD their God, for though I sent them into exile among the nations, I will gather them to their own land, not leaving any behind. I will no longer hide my face from them, for I will pour

out my Spirit on the house of Israel, declares the Sovereign LORD." (**Ezek 39:21-29**)

Following this victory the Lord will complete the return of His people Israel to their land, begun in the early 1900's and made official in 1948. Though He caused them to be scattered all over the world, He'll now bring them back, not leaving any behind. Since about 55% of the world's Jewish people currently live outside of Israel this will be some homecoming. But having witnessed His defeat of their enemies, believing Jews from all over the world will flock to Israel and to Him, yearning for a reinstatement of their Old Covenant relationship. And after waiting for nearly 2000 years for them to return, He's not going to refuse them now. Because of a peace treaty enforced on their behalf by a coming world leader, they'll soon build a Temple, Old Covenant worship being impossible without one. If they follow the instructions from **Ezekiel 40-48** as I believe, they'll build the Temple in Shiloh, about 20 miles north of Jerusalem. This is the Temple that will be made desolate by the anti-Christ and later cleansed at the beginning of the Millennium, just as the second Temple was first made desolate and then cleansed in the time of the Maccabees.

And so this battle will permit the beginning of Daniel's 70th week, the last 7 years of human history before the Millennium. Having given this prophecy to Israel, Ezekiel doesn't get into any detail on its aftermath, especially as is relates to the world's subsequent reactions. But for we who are the Church today, the Battle of **Ezekiel 38-39** carries more significance in what Ezekiel didn't say than in what he did.

Appendix 3

Psalm 83

Psalm 83 was probably written some time after the end of King Solomon's reign (about 900 BC) but the Bible contains no account of such a coordinated effort by all of Israel's neighbors to destroy them, either during that time or since. A partial fulfillment may be in view in **2 Chron. 20** when Moab, Ammon, and parts of Edom invaded Judah during King Jehosophat's reign (872-848 BC) Interestingly, Jahaziel, a Levite who prophesied Judah's victory in that battle was a descendant of Asaph, who wrote **Psalm 83**. Applying one of his favorite tactics, the Lord set Israel's enemies against each other and they defeated themselves. **Ezekiel 38:21** tells of a future use of this same tactic.

But the Battle of **2 Chron. 20** doesn't fully meet the requirements of **Psalm 83**, having many fewer antagonists, so on that basis we'll assume its fulfillment is still in the future, perhaps the very near future. If so, it could be the bridge between the current state of affairs in Israel and the conditions necessary for the Battle of **Ezekiel 38** to happen. Let's find out.

Psalm 83

O God, do not keep silent; be not quiet, O God, be not still. See how your enemies are astir, how your foes rear their heads. With cunning they conspire against your people; they plot against those you cherish.

"Come," they say, "let us destroy them as a nation, that the name of Israel be remembered no more."

With one mind they plot together; they form an alliance against you- the tents of Edom and the Ishmaelites, of Moab and the Hagrites, Gebal, Ammon and Amalek, Philistia, with the people of Tyre. Even Assyria has joined them to lend strength to the descendants of Lot. (**Ps. 83:1-8**)

The language is out of today's headlines and the countries lined up against Israel in this Psalm inhabited the lands of Israel's current neighbors. Edom and the Ishmaelites were in land occupied by southern Jordan today while the territories of Moab and Ammon make up the rest of that country. Ahman, the modern spelling of Ammon, is the capital of Jordan. (While the government of Jordan has a peace treaty with Israel, we should remember that some 70% of Jordan's population is "Palestinian" and in fact the country was originally formed to be the Palestinian home land.).

The Hagrites were part of Aram, whose capitol was Damascus in modern Syria. Gebal (also called Byblos) and Tyre can still be found in present day Lebanon. The Amalekites lived in Israel's southern desert and Philistia settled in Gaza on Israel's southern border. Assyria would conquer Aram shortly after **Psalm 83** was written and the descendants of Lot is another reference to Jordan. Remember, Moab and Ammon were the sons of an incestuous union between Lot and his two daughters.

So here we have all of Israel's next door neighbors, all of them sworn to Israel's destruction, and all of them being whipped into a frenzy by Syria and Iran.

Do to them as you did to Midian, as you did to Sisera and Jabin at the river Kishon, who perished at Endor and became like refuse on the ground. Make their nobles like Oreb and Zeeb, all their princes like Zebah and Zalmunna, who said, "Let us take possession of the pasturelands of God."

Make them like tumbleweed, O my God, like chaff before the wind. As fire consumes the forest or a flame sets the mountains ablaze, so pursue them with your tempest and terrify them with your storm. Cover their faces with shame so that men will seek your name, O LORD. May they ever be ashamed and dismayed; may they perish in disgrace. Let them know that you, whose name is the LORD—that you alone are the Most High over all the earth. (**Psalm 83:9-18**)

Asaph, the Psalm's writer, can't resist telling the Lord exactly how he'd like Israel's enemies to be dealt with. In that sense he's just like you and me.

Midian was defeated by a vastly outnumbered force under the command of Gideon. It was another case of the Lord turning Israel's enemies against each other and causing them to defeat themselves. (**Judges 7**)

Jabin was a king of the Canaanites and Sisera was the commander of his army. The Lord lured the Canaanite army into a trap and the Israelites destroyed them.(**Judges 4**) The commander of Israel's army was named Barak, just like Israel's current Defense Minister. Probably a coincidence.

Oreb, Zeeb Zebah, and Zalmunna were all leaders of the Midianite army defeated by Gideon.

Asaph's prayer was that Israel's current enemies will be just as soundly defeated as were the Midianites and the Canaanites, their armies scattered and their leaders executed.

Thousands of missiles and rockets located in Lebanon, Syria, and Gaza are positioned to strike strategic targets everywhere in Israel. Syria has moved 800 long range missiles into firing positions, placed them on combat readiness, and given them updated target coordinates.

To avoid duplication in targeting, Iran has created and will direct a unified command center in Damascus to coordinate the massive simultaneous deployment of these weapons upon the outbreak of hostilities. Their thought is that the Israelis will not be able to protect themselves against such an all out attack and will be effectively disabled.

But Israel might pick this opportunity to launch a preemptive attack against the command center, wiping out Damascus in fulfillment of **Isaiah 17**. Losing their command and control abilities could cause the enemy attack to degenerate into a confused and chaotic effort that Israel will soundly defeat just like Gideon defeated the Midianites.

Should this be the case, Israel will become larger, not smaller, with the contention over the owner-ship of Gaza, the West bank and the Golan put to an end. Israel will become stronger, not weaker, its military reputation restored and even enhanced. The divided land will be divided no more, and Jerusalem will remain a unified city. The controversial security fence will likely come down, since the borders on all three sides will be safe and the threat of terrorist attacks eliminated. 60 years of war will have finally ended. It will be the perfect opportunity for Israel to be lured into a false sense of security and become a peaceful and unsuspecting people living in a land of unwalled villages as **Ezekiel 38** requires.

Meanwhile, the Russians and Iranians, who will have fought this battle primarily by proxy, will study their defeat and learn from their mistakes, lying in wait for the next opportunity to strike. It won't be long in coming.

Appendix 4

Isaiah 17, An Oracle Concerning Damascus

"See, Damascus will no longer be a city but will become a heap of ruins. The cities of Aroer will be deserted and left to flocks, which will lie down, with no one to make them afraid. **(Isaiah 17:1-2)**

B ecause of the language of these verses, many scholars believe that this prophecy was only partially fulfilled when the Assyrians defeated the Arameans and overran their capital, Damascus, in 732 BC. To this day Damascus is thought to be the world's oldest continuously inhabited city with a 5000-year history and a population close to 2 million, yet **Isaiah 17:1** indicates that it will one day cease to exist.

Some believe the phrase "cities of Aroer" refers to Aramean territory east of the Jordan River around the Arnon River, which flows into the Dead Sea in

97

southern Jordan. However, the Jewish Encyclopedia claims that this phrase in **Isaiah 17:2** is probably translated incorrectly because the geographical distance from Damascus is too great. While they say it's possible that there may have been another Aroer near Damascus, it is more likely that the passage should be rendered "the cities thereof shall be forsaken." If that's the correct translation, it would include the Hezbollah stronghold in the Bekaa Valley of Lebanon, which was part of Aramean territory in Isaiah's time, and is in a direct line between Beirut and Damascus.

The fortified city will disappear from Ephraim, and royal power from Damascus; the remnant of Aram will be like the glory of the Israelites," declares the LORD Almighty. "In that day the glory of Jacob will fade; the fat of his body will waste away. It will be as when a reaper gathers the standing grain and harvests the grain with his arm- as when a man gleans heads of grain in the Valley of Rephaim. (**Isaiah 17:3-5**)

This segment speaks of the defeat of Damascus in 732BC and the destruction of Samaria 10 years later (722 BC). Damascus continued to exist as part of the Assyrian Empire and is still here today, but the ruins of Samaria are just now being excavated out of the sandy soil of Israel.

The systematic relocation of the ruling classes to the far reaches of the Assyrian Empire is also in view here, symbolized by the fat of Jacob's body wasting away. This was standard Assyrian policy to reduce the likelihood of subsequent rebellion among their conquered peoples. Jacob and Ephraim are alternate names for the Northern Kingdom, and Samaria was its capital.

Yet some gleanings will remain, as when an olive tree is beaten, leaving two or three olives on the topmost branches, four or five on the fruitful boughs," *declares the LORD, the God of Israel.* (**Isaiah 17:6**)

Not all the people were dispersed. Farmers were left behind to tend the crops and protect the harvest for their new rulers. They were joined by refugees from other parts of Assyria and their combined descendants were known as the Samaritans in the time of Jesus. (A quick reading of **2 Chronicles 11:16** shows that all the faithful from the 10 northern tribes moved south at the time of the civil war that divided the nation after King Solomon's death 150 years earlier. From then on, all 12 tribes were represented in the Southern Kingdom of Judah, so the 10 tribes from the North weren't totally lost. The Lord has always preserved a believing remnant from all the Tribes of Israel.)

In that day men will look to their Maker and turn their eyes to the Holy One of Israel. They will not look to the altars, the work of their hands, and they will have no regard for the Asherah poles and the incense altars their fingers have made. In that day their strong cities, which they left because of the

Israelites, will be like places abandoned to thickets and undergrowth. And all will be desolation. (**Isaiah 17:7-9**)

This is another passage that's problematic for those who try to consign the whole passage to history. There is simply no reason to believe that the Assyrians turned to God following their conquest of Aram and Israel. And far from abandoning their cities because of the Israelites, it was the Israelites who were defeated and dispersed. The yet future Jewish attack on Damascus causing the destruction and abandonment of Syrian cities, and the eventual return of the survivors to their God is a much more likely fulfillment. And it could happen soon.

You have forgotten God your Savior; you have not remembered the Rock, your fortress. Therefore, though you set out the finest plants and plant imported vines, though on the day you set them out, you make them grow, and on the morning when you plant them, you bring them to bud, yet the harvest will be as nothing in the day of disease and incurable pain. (**Isaiah 17:10-11**)

Asshur, father of the Assyrians, and Aram, father of the Arameans were both sons of Shem. Aram's son Uz is the traditional founder of Damascus. (The setting for Job, the Bible's oldest book, is the Land of Uz.) The knowledge of God in the memories of these patriarchs cannot be questioned. It wasn't that they never knew Him, but that they had forgotten Him, abandoned Him in favor of the Canaanite gods of the region, Baal and his consort Ashtoreth (aka Asherah, Astarte, Ishtar, Aphrodite, Venus.) Currently Syria is almost totally Moslem. Until they return to their Maker and Savior none of their plans and schemes will prosper in the long run, no matter how promising they seem at the beginning.

Oh, the raging of many nations- they rage like the raging sea! Oh, the uproar of the peoples- they roar like the roaring of great waters! Although the peoples roar like the roar of surging waters, when he rebukes them they flee far away, driven before the wind like chaff on the hills, like tumbleweed before a gale. In the evening, sudden terror! Before the morning, they are gone! This is the portion of those who loot us, the lot of those who plunder us. (**Isaiah 17:12-14**)

Having conquered most of the Middle East including the Arameans and the Northern Kingdom, the Assyrians set their sights on the Southern Kingdom, Judah. Assyria's King Sennacherib brought his armies almost literally to the gates of Jerusalem, so close his commanders were within speaking distance of the Jewish defenders. On the night before they were to attack, the Lord sent His angel into the Assyrian camp on Mt. Scopus to slaughter 185,000 Assyrian soldiers. Before dawn they had packed up and fled, ending 44 years of conquest. (**Isaiah 37:36-38**)

This time in Israel's history so parallels the Jewish view of the End Times that Sennacherib is seen by them as a type of the anti-Christ, while Judah's King Hezekiah models the Messiah.

But notice that Isaiah speaks of many nations raging against God's people, not just Assyria, leading us once again to consider Sennacherib's defeat to be a partial fulfillment of Isaiah's prophecy.

The phrase "rushing of many waters" is often used to describe the sound of loud voices and today many nations are stirred up. The cry of anti-Israeli sentiment can be heard around the globe. The various Mid-East "peace" conferences combined with the Gaza war and the boarding of the Turkish/Terrorist flotilla have left Israel standing alone against all but irresistible pressure to negotiate away its very existence. Syria and Iran are dead certain that Israel will attack soon, and are preparing accordingly. Israel's other next-door neighbors are also preparing for war, and indeed many nations are taking sides.

Israel is not blind to these mounting threats, but until lately seems to have been ignoring them. That's about to stop. Israeli Prime Minister Benyamin Netanyahu has repeatedly told the world he will not apologize for defending his country and will continue to do so even if it results in more confrontations. We can easily envision a scenario that escalates into the final fulfillment of **Isaiah 17**, the destruction of Damascus. Once again there will be sudden terror in the evening, and before morning they will be gone.

Appendix 5

The Olivet Discourse
(Matthew 24-25)

The Olivet Discourse is the name scholars have conferred on a private prophecy briefing our Lord gave to Peter, James, John and Andrew on the Mount of Olives. It's recorded in **Matthew 24-25**, **Mark 13-14**, and **Luke 21**. John, while present at the briefing, did not include it in his gospel preferring instead to focus on the time Jesus spent with His disciples in the Upper Room on the night He was betrayed. In reviewing the Olivet Discourse, we'll rely mainly on Matthew's account, it being the most detailed, adding excerpts from Mark and Luke where they add to or clarify the message. And we'll try to stay as close to the Lord's own words as possible to avoid reading any false conclusions into the passage.

As **Matt. 24** opens, Jesus had left the Temple area and was headed for Bethany, where He and the disciples were staying at the home of Mary, Martha, and Lazarus. It was two days before the crucifixion.

Jesus was walking away from the Temple when his disciples came up to him to call his attention to its buildings. "Do you see all these things?" he asked. "I tell you the truth, not one stone here will be left on another; every one will be thrown down."

Later, as Jesus was sitting on the Mount of Olives, the four disciples came to him privately.

Based on His prediction that the Temple would soon be destroyed, they had three questions for the Lord.

1. When will this (Temple destruction) happen?
2. What will be the sign of your (2nd) coming?
3. What will be the sign of the coming of the End of the Age? (**Matt 24:1-3**)

Before we go on, their mindset in asking these questions is critical to our understanding. While the Jews were in Babylon during the 70 year captivity, the angel Gabriel had told Daniel that Israel would be given 490 years from the date they received authorization to rebuild Jerusalem to wrap everything up. (**Daniel 9:24-27**) 483 of those years had past. The Temple had been under construction for nearly 40 years and wasn't finished yet. The disciples were thinking they were nearing the end of the age and now Jesus has said that everything will be torn down. There had never been any talk of a Church Age or a Rapture or of the disciples evangelizing the world. We know about all these things from hindsight, but they were probably in a state of great distress when they came to Him. Remember, they were Jewish men, familiar with Jewish history, and asking about Israel's future.

Even after the Resurrection they still didn't understand. This is confirmed by the question they asked Jesus on the Mount of Olives after the resurrection. *"Lord, are you now going to restore the Kingdom?"* (**Acts 1:6**)

It wasn't clear until James explained it 20 years later at the Council of Jerusalem. (**Acts 15:13-18**). He said the Lord was first going to take from among the gentiles a people for Himself (the Church). After that He would turn again to Israel.

OK, back to our study. In the Matthew account the Lord ignored the first question and went straight to question 2. So for His answer to question 1 we'll go to **Luke 21** where it's contained. Having begun like Matthew with an account of the End Times in verses 10-12, Luke backtracks to their first question in verses 12-24.

"But before all this, they will lay hands on you and persecute you. They will deliver you to synagogues and prisons, and you will be brought before kings and governors, and all on account of my name. This will result in your being witnesses to them. But make up your mind not to worry beforehand how you will defend yourselves. For I will give you words and wisdom that none of your adversaries will be able to resist or contradict. You will be betrayed even by parents, brothers, relatives and friends, and they will put

some of you to death. All men will hate you because of me. But not a hair of your head will perish. By standing firm you will gain life." (**Luke 21:12-19**)

Having told them what the rest of their lives would be like, and that their eternal destiny with Him was assured, the Lord finally answered their question about the Temple destruction.

"When you see Jerusalem being surrounded by armies, you will know that its desolation is near. Then let those who are in Judea flee to the mountains, let those in the city get out, and let those in the country not enter the city. For this is the time of punishment in fulfillment of all that has been written. How dreadful it will be in those days for pregnant women and nursing mothers! There will be great distress in the land and wrath against this people. They will fall by the sword and will be taken as prisoners to all the nations. Jerusalem will be trampled on by the Gentiles until the times of the Gentiles are fulfilled. (**Luke 21:20-24**)

In what appears to be poor advice, He told them to get out of town when they saw the city being surrounded by enemy troops, an event that took place nearly 40 years later. The objective of a besieging army was to trap everyone inside so the plight of starving women and children would have a discouraging influence on the leadership. Non-combatants were not allowed free passage through enemy lines for this reason.

But a strange thing happened in the siege of Jerusalem. After surrounding the city, the Roman army was suddenly told to abandon their position and prepare for an immediate departure to Rome. General Titus, who commanded the army, was the son of Vespasian, a man striving to become the Roman Emperor. Fearing he would need extra help in consolidating his power, Vespasian ordered Titus to bring the army home to assist. But before they could depart, another message arrived saying that all was in order and to resume the siege of Jerusalem. For one week the siege lines had been abandoned, and during this time Christians who heeded the Lord's earlier warning escaped. Although 1.2 million Jews died in Rome's defeat of Israel, according to the historian Josephus not one Christian perished in the siege of Jerusalem. The Lord's advice had been sound and even strategically clever.

Roman soldiers were paid from the valuables they confiscated in battle, and the Temple was a huge prize. Titus wanted to preserve it, which would have deprived the soldiers of a tremendous bonus. Defending the Temple entrance with his sword raised against his own troops, he watched helplessly as a flaming torch was thrown over his head into the Temple starting a fire. The ensuing blaze generated such heat that the gold plating covering the wooden plank ceiling began to melt and run down the stone walls, seeping into the cracks between the stones. When the blaze was finally extinguished, the soldiers dismantled the ruined walls to get the gold. By the time they had finished, not one stone was left standing on another, graphically fulfilling the Lord's prophecy to His disciples.

Now, let's go back to **Matthew 24** for the Lord's answers to their other questions, picking up the narrative in verse 4.

Jesus answered: *"Watch out that no one deceives you. For many will come in my name, claiming, 'I am the Christ,' and will deceive many. You will hear of wars and rumors of wars, but see to it that you are not alarmed. Such things must happen, but the end is still to come. Nation will rise against nation, and kingdom against kingdom. There will be famines and earthquakes in various places. All these are the beginning of birth pains.* (**Matt 24:4-9**)

The coming Church Age would be characterized by the appearance of false messiahs, conflict between nations, natural disasters, and famine. Luke adds pestilence and great signs from heaven to the mix (**Luke 21:11**), as does the King James Version of Matthew. The comparison to birth pains reveals that while these events would occur all through the Church Age, they would be more and more frequent and more intense as the end comes nearer.

"Then you will be handed over to be persecuted and put to death, and you will be hated by all nations because of me. At that time many will turn away from the faith and will betray and hate each other, and many false prophets will appear and deceive many people. Because of the increase of wickedness, the

love of most will grow cold, but he who stands firm to the end will be saved. And this gospel of the kingdom will be preached in the whole world as a testimony to all nations, and then the end will come. (**Matt 24:9-14**)

The words here are very similar to those in **Luke 21:20-24**, but in Matthew the focus is clearly the End Times. It helps to remember that verses 4-14 are an overview of the End Times that cover the period from the beginning of the birth pangs to the 2nd Coming. Believers will be severely persecuted at the End of the Age (Matthew's version) just like they were at the beginning (Luke's version) and because Tribulation believers are not promised Eternal Security like the Church was, many will turn away from the faith due to the intense persecution. Before the Lord's return, the Good News will be preached in every nation to prepare the people of Earth for His coming and to deny them a plausible excuse for rejecting Him, or pleading ignorance. **Rev. 14:6-7** contains the fulfill-ment of this promise.

"So when you see standing in the holy place 'the abomination that causes desolation,' spoken of through the prophet Daniel—let the reader under-stand— then let those who are in Judea flee to the mountains. Let no one on the roof of his house go down to take anything out of the house. Let no one in the field go back to get his cloak. How dreadful it will be in those days for pregnant women and nursing mothers! Pray that your flight will not take

*place in winter or on the Sabbath. For then there will
be great distress, unequaled from the beginning of
the world until now–and never to be equaled again.*
(Matt 24:15-21)

In this portion the Lord backed up to pinpoint
the beginning of the Great Tribulation, a time of
judgment whose very name comes from here (translated in the NIV as great distress), one that will sur-
pass anything the world has ever seen. The Prophet
Daniel had written of a time in the future when the
Temple would be desecrated by an event he called
"the Abomination that causes Desolation" **(Daniel
9:24-27)** and the Lord was now informing them that
this event would trigger the Great Tribulation.

Since Daniel's time something like it had
only happened once. In 168 BC the Syrian Ruler
Antiochus Epiphanes (the name means God made
manifest), after muscling his way into Israel, seized
the Temple and converted it to pagan worship. He
erected a statue of Zeus in the Holy Place in his own
likeness, requiring everyone to bow down before it
on pain of death. The Jews called this desecration
the Abomination that causes Desolation, borrowing
language from **Daniel 9:27**. It so angered them that
they rose up in arms against the Syrian invaders. The
3 1/2 year long Maccabean Revolt, as it was called,
resulted in the Syrians' expulsion from Israel and a
Temple cleansing and re-dedication ceremony that's
still memorialized annually in the Feast of Hanukkah.

Today, students of the End Times see a fright-
eningly clear model of the Great Tribulation in the

Maccabean Revolt, with a foreign invader calling himself God and demanding worship, a Temple desecration, and unbelievable persecution ending in a 3 1/2-year war of liberation. As we'll see that's just what the Lord intended in mentioning Daniel's Prophecy.

193 years after the Maccabean Revolt, Jesus spoke of the Abomination that causes Desolation as something still in the future. And a careful reading of his 70 weeks prophecy shows that Daniel placed it in the middle of the 70th week, long after both the Messiah's arrival and rejection, and the destruction of the city and sanctuary. Since nothing like this has happened since the Lord gave His warning, it means that one day soon another foreign invader will muscle his way into Israel, calling himself God and demanding worship.

There'll be another Temple desecration, and more unbelievable persecution ending in another war of liberation, only this time the entire planet will be affected, not just Israel. According to Daniel, it will begin half way through the last 7 years of human history establishing its duration as 3 1/2 years just like it's earlier model. In **2 Thes, 2:4** Paul expanded Daniel's account, connecting it to the antichrist at the End of the Age. These things confirm that the sacrilege that kicked off the Maccabean Revolt serves as a preview to help people recognize the sacrilege that will kick off the Great Tribulation. (See also **Rev. 13:14-17**)

There are three factors here that underscore the "Jewishness" of the Lord's warning. First there will be a desecration of their Temple, second the warning is given specifically to those in Judea, the region of Jerusalem in Israel, and third there's an admonition to pray that it won't happen on the Sabbath, a day when Jewish law forbids traveling. Clearly the Lord was saying that there will be a nation of Jewish people observing His Law in Israel at the End of the Age and they will have rebuilt their Temple prior to His return. (For more on the coming Temple see Appendix 7 at the back of this book.)

If those days had not been cut short, no one would survive, but for the sake of the elect those days will be shortened. At that time if anyone says to you, 'Look, here is the Christ!' or, 'There he is!' do not believe it. For false Christs and false prophets will appear and perform great signs and miracles to deceive even the elect—if that were possible. See, I have told you ahead of time.

"So if anyone tells you, 'There he is, out in the desert,' do not go out; or, 'Here he is, in the inner rooms,' do not believe it. For as lightning that comes from the east is visible even in the west, so will be the coming of the Son of Man. Wherever there is a carcass, there the vultures will gather. (**Matt. 24:22-28**)

The Great Tribulation is the most specifically documented span of time in all of Scripture. In one place we're told it's 3 1/2 years long (time, times and half a time; one year plus two years plus half a year as in **Rev. 12:14**), in another 42 months (**Rev. 11:2**) and in still another 1260 days (**Rev.12:6**). Use the original calendar for Earth, 12 months of 30 days each for a 360 day year, and you find all three measurements identical from a time standpoint.

Moreover there isn't a single hint anywhere that it will be of a shorter duration. Most scholars who read the passage above literally, conclude that the phrase cut short means that for the sake of His elect the Lord will step in on the 1260th day and put an end to the warfare instead of letting it run to its logical conclusion; the destruction of every human on the planet.

"Immediately after the distress of those days, " 'the sun will be darkened, and the moon will not give its light; the stars will fall from the sky, and the heavenly bodies will be shaken.' At that time the sign of the Son of Man will appear in the sky, and all the nations of the earth will mourn. They will see the Son of Man coming on the clouds of the sky, with power and great glory. And he will send his angels with a loud trumpet call, and they will gather his elect from the four winds, from one end of the heavens to the other. (**Matt.24:29-31**)

In bringing the Great Tribulation to an end, the Lord will cause the Sun and Moon to be darkened. Then His sign will appear in the sky, and finally He Himself will come in power and glory just as He promised Caiaphas, the High Priest, at His trial 2000 years ago (**Matt. 26:64**). All the nations will mourn because His appearance rings the closing bell for the time of salvation. Too late, the people of Earth will realize that He is just Who He's always claimed to be, and they've missed their last chance to be saved.

At His signal, His angels will gather His elect (believers) from all over Heaven to return with Him to Earth to establish His Kingdom. This is one of two vague hints in the Olivet Discourse that there'll be a body of believers in Heaven awaiting His 2nd coming. According to Mark's account, surviving believers on earth will also be summoned (**Mark 13:27**) to witness His triumphant return.

"Now learn this lesson from the fig tree: As soon as its twigs get tender and its leaves come out, you know that summer is near. Even so, when you see all these things, you know that it is near, right at the door. I tell you the truth, this generation will certainly not pass away until all these things have happened. Heaven and earth will pass away, but my words will never pass away. (**Matt. 24:32-36**)

The fig tree is the last to bud, so when it does we know Summer's almost here. Through His disciples, the Lord told the people on Earth at the End of the Age that when all these things begin to happen, it means the end is very near. Indeed, of the 6000 year history of Man only 3 1/2 will remain.

The Greek word translated generation also means race, and can be interpreted as the Lord's promise that the Jewish race wouldn't be extinguished before the End comes. And that's remarkably true. The vicious and oft repeated attempts to rid the world of its Jewry have all failed, and Israel has risen from the grave after a 2000-year absence to once again become the focus of world attention.

Yet there's also a sense in which the Lord's promise can be rendered, "I tell you the truth, the generation that sees the beginning of these signs will also see their culmination." In other words, they will all be concluded during the lifetimes of those being born as they begin. There's precedent for this too. All the prophecies concerning the Lord's first visit were fulfilled within the lifespan of the generation into which He was born.

Please note that if this view is the correct one, as I believe it to be, the Lord didn't promise that, once they begin, all End Times prophecies would be fulfilled before the next generation is born, but only that they would be fulfilled during the lifetimes of those being born at their commencement. A Biblical generation is nominally 40 years, but a lifetime is more like 70 (**Psalm 90:10, Isaiah 23:15**). The folks who added 40 years to Israel's 1948 rebirth and predicted the Rapture would happen in 1988 were off on two counts. first, they should have added a lifetime, not the length of a biblical generation, and second, it's the 2nd Coming that will happen within a lifetime of the first signs. The Rapture could happen at any time prior to that.

"No one knows about that day or hour, not even the angels in heaven, nor the Son, but only the Father. As it was in the days of Noah, so it will be at the coming of the Son of Man. For in the days before

the flood, people were eating and drinking, marrying and giving in marriage, up to the day Noah entered the ark; and they knew nothing about what would happen until the flood came and took them all away. That is how it will be at the coming of the Son of Man. Two men will be in the field; one will be taken and the other left. Two women will be grinding with a hand mill; one will be taken and the other left. (**Matt 24:36-41**)

Don't let this passage confuse you like it has so many others. Note that the first sentence reads, "No one knows about that day or hour." Plenty of people on Earth at the End of the Age will know the Lord is due to return. Remember, both the kick-off event and duration of the Great Tribulation are clearly and unmistakably described. On the day when the anti-christ stands in the Temple and declares that he's God they'll just have to count off 1260 days to know when the time of judgment will end. Also, they'll see the Sun and Moon turn dark and stars fall out of the sky. That's the signal that the Great Tribulation has ended (**Matt 24:29**). Then the Lord's sign will appear in the sky (**Matt. 24:30**) And finally they'll see the Lord Himself coming in the clouds in power and glory. But the period of time required between the end of the Great Tribulation and the completion of this sequence is anybody's guess, and that's what this passage says.

Also the Lord compared the time of His return to the time of Noah, so we should expect to find similar circumstances leading up to these two events. And we do. Both involve worldwide judgments that occur at a time when most people are caught unaware. Although in both cases the people of Earth are given repeated warnings of what's coming, those warnings are ignored by almost everyone. In the case of the Great Flood, judgment came in the form of rain, which fell on the Earth for 40 days and 40 nights. In the case of the Great Tribulation 21 separate judgment events unfold over a 3 1/2 year period. This is why although only 8 people survived the Flood, the Lord warned that the Great Tribulation would be the worst time of judgment in human history.

Also, both the Great Flood and the Great Tribulation have three components; judgment, preservation through judgment, and escape from judgment. In the Days of Noah, the unbelievers were judged, Noah's family was preserved through the judgment, and Enoch escaped it altogether. At the End of the Age, unbelievers are judged, the remnant of Israel is preserved through the judgment, and the Church escapes from judgment.

Now let's consider those words "taken" and "left" in **Matt. 24:40-41** a little more closely. The Greek word translated taken literally means received, and the one translated left means put away. They refer to the disposition of those remaining alive on Earth when the Lord returns, the Tribulation Survivors. Those who've become believers will be received into the Kingdom, and those who haven't will be put away into the place prepared for the devil and his angels. Folks who try to find the rapture of the church in these words are simply looking in the wrong place.

"Therefore keep watch, because you do not know on what day your Lord will come. But understand this: If the owner of the house had known at what time of night the thief was coming, he would have kept watch and would not have let his house be broken into. So you also must be ready, because the Son of Man will come at an hour when you do not expect him. (**Matt. 24:42-44**)

This warning is given primarily to those Tribulation Survivors who are not believers. As I stated above, once the Great Tribulation begins, all believers on Earth will know when it will end. The sequence of events that follow is also clear. The only thing they won't know is the exact day and hour of His Coming.

No, this warning is to the undecided, who aren't counting up the prophecies being fulfilled around them, and don't realize that if they waver too long, they'll be taken by surprise and miss their last chance at salvation. Don't get me wrong, they'll be only too aware of the massive disruptions to their lives caused by the End Times judgments. They just won't understand what's behind it all. Remember, confusion and deception will be the order of the day.

Think about the analogy of the thief. As the Lord returns unexpectedly (like a thief) He'll be breaking into a place the enemy thinks belongs to him and his followers. *"Their destiny is destruction, their god is their stomach, and their glory is in their shame. Their mind is on earthly things. But our citizenship is in heaven. And we eagerly await a Savior from there, the Lord Jesus Christ."* (**Phil 3:19-20**) He won't be coming as a thief in the night as far as believers are concerned, stealthily breaking into their world. They'll be eagerly watching and impatiently waiting, counting the days, praying for His coming, longing for Him to take them home to be with Him forever.

Beginning in **Matt. 24:45** and continuing through the end of chapter 25, Matthew recounts three parables, the Faithful Servant, the Ten Bridesmaids and the Talents. There's also a warning to Tribulation Survivors, the Sheep and Goat judgment. In each one the emphasis is on separating the faithful from the unfaithful following the Lord's return. The faithful will be received with honors into His Kingdom, while the unfaithful are put away to be judged. Since they all include a reference to time that places them in the aftermath of His 2nd coming, the entire chapter expands on the "taken and left" statement of **Matt. 24:40-41**.

Because there's been so much confusion, let's make this perfectly clear. Of all the views on the timing of the Rapture of the Church, none place it after the 2nd coming. But look how clearly that time frame is indicated in each portion of **Matt. 25**. Backing up a little to establish the order, we read;

"Immediately after the distress of those days," signs in the Heavens after the end of the Great Tribulation (**Matt 24:29**)

"At that time," His appearance in the sky after the end of the Great Tribulation (**Matt. 24:30**)

"No one knows about that day," the day of the 2nd Coming, after the Tribulation (**Matt: 24:36**)

"At that time," connecting the parable of the ten virgins to the 2nd Coming (**Matt 25:1**)

"Again," referring to the same time frame in beginning the parable of the talents (**Matt. 25:14**)

"When the Son of Man comes in all His Glory," beginning the Sheep and Goat judgment which describes the judgment of Tribulation Survivors after the 2nd Coming (**Matt 25:31**).

As you see, they all occur chronologically after the Tribulation and 2nd Coming, and all describe the situation on Earth following the Lord's return. Therefore none of them can be used to describe the Rapture or any other aspect of the Church. The Church Age ends with the Rapture and that occurs well before the 2nd Coming.

With that introduction, let's look at the parables of the Olivet Discourse.

The Parable Of The Servants
Who then is the faithful and wise servant, whom the master has put in charge of the servants in his household to give them their food at the proper time? It will be good for that servant whose master finds him doing so when he returns. I tell you the truth, he will put him in charge of all his possessions.

But suppose that servant is wicked and says to himself, 'My master is staying away a long time,' and he then begins to beat his fellow servants and to eat and drink with drunkards. The master of that servant will come on a day when he does not expect him and at an hour he is not aware of. He will cut him to pieces and assign him a place with the hypocrites, where there will be weeping and gnashing of teeth. (**Matt. 24:45-51**)

The Lord's brother issued a stern warning in **James 3:1** that not many should presume to be teachers because those who teach will be judged more strictly. The worst punishment is always reserved for those in charge, heads of organized religious groups who, instead of "feeding" their flocks with the Bread of Life and encouraging them with the promise of the Lord's return, will oppress them with legalistic requirements (beat them) and confuse and deceive them with false doctrines that deny the validity of God's prophetic Word (eat and drink with drunkards). By their actions they will demonstrate the depravity of their own souls, showing themselves to be devoid of the Holy Spirit and worthy of punishment. Knowingly or not, they're infiltrators from the enemy's camp. Paul described false teachers as Satan's servants disguised as servants of righteousness. (**2 Cor. 11:14**)

Having forsaken the truth they no will longer be watching for the Lord's return, ignoring the obvious fulfillment of prophecy all around them and ridiculing those whose child-like faith sustains them. They are the worst enemy because they'll look and sound like friends. They're like the one John describes as appearing to have the authority of the Lamb but who speaks the words of the Dragon (**Rev. 13:11**).

But the Lord will elevate to a place of authority in His Kingdom those who will have kept the word of God through the intense hardship and persecution of the times, and will have taught sound doctrine to the flocks entrusted to them. Just as some among the common folk alive when the Lord returns will be received into the Kingdom with honors, while others are put away in everlasting shame and contempt, so it will be with their leaders.

The Parable Of The 10 Virgins

"At that time the kingdom of heaven will be like ten virgins who took their lamps and went out to meet the bridegroom. Five of them were foolish and five were wise. The foolish ones took their lamps but did not take any oil with them. The wise, however, took oil in jars along with their lamps. The bridegroom was a long time in coming, and they all became drowsy and fell asleep.

"At midnight the cry rang out: 'Here's the bride-groom! Come out to meet him!'

"Then all the virgins woke up and trimmed their lamps. The foolish ones said to the wise, 'Give us some of your oil; our lamps are going out.' " 'No,' they replied, 'there may not be enough for both us

and you. Instead, go to those who sell oil and buy some for yourselves.'

"But while they were on their way to buy the oil, the bridegroom arrived. The virgins who were ready went in with him to the wedding banquet. And the door was shut.

"Later the others also came. 'Sir! Sir!' they said. 'Open the door for us!'

"But he replied, 'I tell you the truth, I don't know you.'

"Therefore keep watch, because you do not know the day or the hour. (**Matt. 25:1-13**)

The clearest indication of the Tribulation believer's exposure is found in the Parable of the 10 Virgins. The timing of this parable is identified as just following the 2nd Coming, since the phrase "at that time" refers back the the day and hour of His Coming (**Matt. 24:36**). The 10 virgins are all on Earth waiting for the Bridegroom (Jesus) to return. All 10 have both lamps and oil at the beginning, indicating that all were once saved. (When oil is used symbolically it always refers to the Holy Spirit.)

The five who ran out of oil symbolize Tribulation believers who let their faith lapse by not remaining spiritually awake and alert. At the end they wake up, discover their peril, and rush about trying to renew their faith. While they're working to get back into a right relationship with Jesus, He returns and the door to salvation is closed to them forever. Remember, all 10 virgins are caught sleeping when He returns. They all behaved badly. It's the oil that distinguishes one group from the other, not their behavior.

Some try to make this into a parable about the Church, always symbolized by a bride. There is a similarity between virgin and bride due to the fact that in those days brides were nearly always virgins. But so were all of their unmarried friends. The Greek word simply means "someone who has never had sexual intercourse". When used in connection with the Church the word is always singular, such as in **2 Cor 11:2**. *"For I am jealous for you with a godly jealousy; for I betrothed you to one husband, so that to Christ I might present you as a pure virgin."* Paul spoke of one virgin. Here there are 10 of them. While the word has often been translated as bridesmaids in this parable, these 10 virgins are never called the Bride.

Through out the parable, no bride is ever mentioned, and certainly could not be excluded by her husband from the wedding banquet, or Seudas Mitzvah, a festive meal that follows the wedding ceremony. None of these 10 made it to the actual marriage ceremony, oil or not, so none of them can be the bride. The timing, the grammar, and the context all testify against interpreting this parable as a warning to the Church. The 10 virgins represent Tribulation survivors trying to gain entrance to the Messianic Kingdom, or Millennium. Some will have maintained their faith and be welcomed in. the others will not and will be refused admittance.

The parable ends with the warning, *"Therefore keep watch, because you do not know the day or the hour."* (**Matt 25:13**) This is the fourth such warning in the span of 28 verses, all dealing with the time of His 2nd coming. Tribulation believers must remain alert at all times and guard their position carefully. It will take a tremendous amount of faith to sustain oneself through this time, and each believer is responsible for keeping his or her own faith strong.

Some try to say that since the Lord warned them about the day and hour being unknown, He must be talking about the Rapture. After all, won't people be able to count off 1260 days from the Abomination of Desolation to the 2nd Coming? It turns out that it's not quite that easy. The Great Tribulation will last 1260 days, it's true, and immediately afterward the Sun will be darkened, the Moon not give its light, and stars will fall from the sky. (**Matt. 24:29**) This will be the signal that the Great Tribulation has ended.

Next the sign of the Son of Man will appear in the sky. The Greek word for sign means that a symbol or token will appear alerting people of a coming event. Sometime after the sign appears, people will see Him coming on the clouds. So there's a sequence of events that will take place, one following the other. But we're not told the duration of any one of them. Imagine the suspense that will create on Earth, knowing that the End has come but not knowing exactly when the Lord will actually return. By the signs, they'll know He's due, but they won't know the day or hour.

Daniel 12:12 says that 1335 days will elapse between the beginning of the Great Tribulation and the beginning of the Millennium. Somewhere in the 75 days between the last day of the Tribulation (#1260) and the first day of the Kingdom (#1335), the Lord will return, but nobody will know exactly when.

Personally, I think that the 10 virgins represent people on Earth who will awaken when they see His sign in the sky, and will know that the Bridegroom is coming. That's when some of them will realize that their faith has lapsed and will begin frantically trying to prepare themselves. But alas, He comes before they're ready and it's too late.

The Parable Of The Talents
"Again, it will be like a man going on a journey, who called his servants and entrusted his property to them. To one he gave five talents of money, to another two talents, and to another one talent, each according to his ability. Then he went on his journey. The man who had received the five talents went at once and put his money to work and gained five more. So also, the one with the two talents gained two more. But the man who had received the one talent went off, dug a hole in the ground and hid his master's money.

"After a long time the master of those servants returned and settled accounts with them. The man who had received the five talents brought the other

five. 'Master,' he said, 'you entrusted me with five talents. See, I have gained five more.' "His master replied, 'Well done, good and faithful servant! You have been faithful with a few things; I will put you in charge of many things. Come and share your master's happiness!'

"The man with the two talents also came. 'Master,' he said, 'you entrusted me with two talents; see, I have gained two more.' "His master replied, 'Well done, good and faithful servant! You have been faithful with a few things; I will put you in charge of many things. Come and share your master's happiness!'

"Then the man who had received the one talent came. 'Master,' he said, 'I knew that you are a hard man, harvesting where you have not sown and gathering where you have not scattered seed. So I was afraid and went out and hid your talent in the ground. See, here is what belongs to you.'

"His master replied, 'You wicked, lazy servant! So you knew that I harvest where I have not sown and gather where I have not scattered seed? Well then, you should have put my money on deposit with the bankers, so that when I returned I would have received it back with interest.

"'Take the talent from him and give it to the one who has the ten talents. For everyone who has will be given more, and he will have an abundance. Whoever does not have, even what he has will be taken from him.

And throw that worthless servant outside, into the darkness, where there will be weeping and gnashing of teeth.' (**Matt. 25:14-30**)

In **Matt 25:14**, at the beginning of the Parable of the Talents, the word "again" means the Lord is giving another illustration from the same time period as the parable of the 10 Virgins, the Day of His Coming. That means it takes place on Earth after the 2nd Coming, whereas the Church is to be judged in Heaven after the Rapture. Though the English word talent, which is a gift or ability, comes from this parable, in those days a talent was either a Greek unit of measure (about 75 pounds), or a coin worth in excess of $1,000. The key to interpreting a parable is knowing that everything is symbolic of something else, so in this parable a talent represents something valuable to the Lord that he wished to have managed in His absence. Upon his return, He asks those to whom he had entrusted it what they've accomplished.

Reading the Bible, it's clear that money isn't important to the Lord. But **Psalm 138:2** says that He values His Word above all else. I believe the talents represent His Word. Those who sow it into the hearts of others find that it multiplies in new believers. Those who study it find that their own understanding grows, multiplying their faith.

But those who ignore His word find that it's like burying it in the ground. Out of sight, out of mind, until what little they began with is lost to them. Even though they held themselves out to be the Lord's servants, this proves His word never held any value for them, and condemns them to be cast into the outer darkness. They knew the truth but buried it. Now He's come back and it's too late.

No matter how famous a teacher he or she might be, don't ever let any one try to persuade you that this parable is about the gifts the Lord gives the Church and our responsibility to use them or be judged. It just isn't so. The timing is wrong, the location is wrong, the context is wrong, and the punishment for disobedience is wrong.

The Sheep And Goat Judgment

"When the Son of Man comes in his glory, and all the angels with him, he will sit on his throne in heavenly glory. All the nations will be gathered before him, and he will separate the people one from another as a shepherd separates the sheep from the goats. He will put the sheep on his right and the goats on his left.

"Then the King will say to those on his right, 'Come, you who are blessed by my Father; take your inheritance, the kingdom prepared for you since the creation of the world. For I was hungry and you gave me something to eat, I was thirsty and you gave me something to drink, I was a stranger and you invited me in, I needed clothes and you clothed me, I was sick and you looked after me, I was in prison and you came to visit me.'

"Then the righteous will answer him, 'Lord, when did we see you hungry and feed you, or thirsty and

give you something to drink? When did we see you a stranger and invite you in, or needing clothes and clothe you? When did we see you sick or in prison and go to visit you?' "The King will reply, 'I tell you the truth, whatever you did for one of the least of these brothers of mine, you did for me.'

"Then he will say to those on his left, 'Depart from me, you who are cursed, into the eternal fire prepared for the devil and his angels. For I was hungry and you gave me nothing to eat, I was thirsty and you gave me nothing to drink, I was a stranger and you did not invite me in, I needed clothes and you did not clothe me, I was sick and in prison and you did not look after me.'

"They also will answer, 'Lord, when did we see you hungry or thirsty or a stranger or needing clothes or sick or in prison, and did not help you?'

"He will reply, 'I tell you the truth, whatever you did not do for one of the least of these, you did not do for me.'

"Then they will go away to eternal punishment, but the righteous to eternal life." (**Matt. 25:31-46**)

Matt. 25:31 leaves no doubt as to the timing on this one. It begins "When the Son of Man comes ... " and goes on to talk about the Lord setting up His throne on Earth after His return for the Judgment of the Nations, actually a judgment of Gentile tribulation survivors. The Lord doesn't judge nations in the eternal sense, only individuals. The Greek word here is ethnos, and means "people of every kind." They'll be judged by how they treated "His brothers" during the Great Tribulation. It's called the Sheep and Goat judgment, with the sheep representing those who helped His brothers through the horrific times just past and goats being those who didn't.

Some say His brothers are believers, whether Jew or Gentile, and others say they're specifically Jews, but the most important point is that these tribulation survivors aren't being judged by their works. Their works are being cited as evidence of their faith, as in **James 2:18**. To give aid to a believer, especially a Jew, during the Great Tribulation will take even more courage than it did in Hitler's Germany, and will be an offense punishable by death. Only a follower of Jesus would dare do it or even want to. Those who helped "His brothers" will have demonstrated their faith by their works and will be ushered live into the Kingdom. Those who refused to help will have condemned themselves to the eternal fires by this evidence of their lack of faith.

All four of these illustrations teach the same lesson. Faithful Tribulation believers will go live into the Kingdom while those who don't maintain their righteousness will be escorted off the planet with their unbelieving counterparts.

What's The Point?

It seems clear then, that salvation in the post church period will be a much more tenuous situation than the one we enjoy, devoid of any guarantees and requiring great personal responsibility in the face of devastating judgments and relentless persecution. Even though evidence of God's existence will abound in the judgments that regularly shake the Earth to its very foundations, maintaining one's faith during this time will be no small task. This realization adds great meaning to the Lord's promise to Church Age believers. *"Blessed are those who have not seen and yet have believed."* (**John 20:29**)

It's clear that the only questions the Lord answered in the Olivet Discourse are the three the disciples asked. "When will these things happen? What will be the sign of your coming and of the End of the Age?" Having chosen to delay the announcement of the Rapture of the Church until nearly 20 years after His resurrection, the Lord neither taught it to His disciples nor, as we've seen, did He address it in the Olivet Discourse. No, the Olivet Discourse was a summary of Jewish Eschatology given to Jews in Israel, before the birth of the Church, and only vaguely hinting at its existence.

So in coming to the end of our commentary we're left with one big unanswered question. Why didn't the Lord teach something as important as the Doctrine of the Rapture to his disciples? Obviously there's a good reason and I'll explain it now.

In 51 AD, almost 20 years after the Resurrection, the Apostle Paul became the first to reveal the incredible secret that would become known as the Rapture of the Church. He did this in his earliest written communication, his first letter to the Thessalonians (**1**

Thes. 4:16-17), repeating it four years later in a letter to the Corinthians (**1 Cor. 15:51-53**). In doing so, Paul finally identified the group mentioned in **Matt. 24:31** who would be in Heaven waiting to return with the Lord at his 2nd coming.

From **1 Thessalonians 4:16-17** we know that, at the Rapture, the dead in Christ will rise first to be followed immediately by believers who are left and still alive. Concerning living believers, Paul's letter to the Corinthians explains that in the twinkling of an eye, we'll be changed from mortal to immortal, bypassing death altogether (**1 Cor.15:51-53**). Either way, in less than an instant we'll all arrive together in Heaven. Because everyone who believes in the Rapture of the Church agrees it will take place sometime before the 2nd coming, the group in Heaven that the Lord sends His angels to gather up in **Matt 24:31** has to include resurrected and raptured church age believers.

As an aside, those who dispute this doctrine claim that the word rapture doesn't appear in the English translation of either of Paul's letters cited above (nor anywhere else in scripture for that matter) and of course they're correct. The original Greek word Paul used to describe the rapture in 1 Thes. 4:17 is harpazo, usually rendered "caught up" in English translations.

Because of the growing dominance of the Roman Empire in Biblical times, Latin was fast replacing Greek as the world's common language and so about 400 AD the Bible was translated from Hebrew and Greek into Latin. Harpazo became raptus, the Latin root of the English word rapture. It means "the transporting of a person from one place to another, especially to heaven." So it's the Latin version that gave the event its name. Our current English translations are taken directly from the earlier Greek texts, and that's why the word rapture doesn't appear in them.

Why The Delay?

But why didn't the Lord announce the whole issue of salvation for the Gentiles including the Rapture of the Church during his time here? Two reasons. First, Israel had to receive a bona fide offer of the Kingdom. His commitment to them was clear. The first time He sent the disciples out to minister, He told them, *"Do not go among the Gentiles or enter any town of the Samaritans"* (**Matt. 10:5**). And later when the disciples asked Him to respond to a Gentile woman whose daughter needed healing, He at first declined saying, *"I was sent only to the lost sheep of Israel"* (**Matt. 15:23-24**). Before He could expand His ministry to the Gentiles, He had to fulfill His promise to Israel.

So just as he had offered reconciliation to the Amorites in Abraham's time, knowing in advance that they would reject Him, (**Gen. 15:16**) the Lord extended His offer of a Kingdom to Israel. And of course Israel did reject His offer by attributing the power behind His miracles to Satan, (**Matt. 12:22-37**) and eventually accusing Him of blasphemy (**Matt. 26:65**). This rejection was confirmed to them in the parable of the tenants (**Matt. 21:13-44**). But the pre-determined order of first the Jew then the Gentile (**Rom. 1:16**) had to be observed. (Prophetic

Scriptures tell us Israel will get another chance, and the next time they'll accept.)

Second, knowing before history began that the Jews would reject Him the first time, the Lord had always planned to extend His offer of salvation to the Gentiles, and that meant something really dramatic had to happen. Gentiles were even worse sinners than Jews, who at least made periodic attempts to obey. But for 4000 years the Lord had demonstrated through His people that no level of excellence in human behavior could ever meet His requirements for salvation. And even with the most complex religious system ever devised, the most expensive house of worship ever built, the most detail conscious people ever created, and the most aggressive sacrifice of innocent blood ever undertaken, the final score at the end of the Dispensation of Law was zero souls saved through religious works. (**Rom. 3:20**)

At Least Somebody's Listening

Well, He didn't convince them but He did convince Satan, who believed that eventually all of humanity would wind up with him in the lost column of the ledger, Jew and Gentile alike. Surely then the Lord would have to rescind his judgment against Satan (**Isaiah 14:16-21**). After all, was he any worse than sinful mankind? Hadn't they also rebelled, tried to set up their own kingdoms, and even tried to become their own God? The God Who is Love couldn't stand by and let all his precious children go to hell just to punish Satan, could He? And if He bent the rules for them, He'd have to bend for Satan.

Surprise, Surprise

But no one knew what the Lord had cooked up to solve this problem. Having known from the beginning that we couldn't save ourselves by our works, He had determined in advance that He would save us by our faith. That meant someone qualified to do so would have to step up and pay the penalty for our sins for us. Then God could promise us that if we accepted this substitution in faith, we would be saved.

Of course the only One qualified to do this for us was God Himself. So He did. He Who had no sin was made a sin offering for us, so that in Him we might become the righteousness of God. (**2 Cor. 5:21**) And as a special blessing for "believing though we have not seen" (**John 20:29**) He even went so far as to make His Church a separate classification of humanity, (**Ephe. 2:15**) giving us a pre-imminent place in His Kingdom, and promising to take us out of this world to be with Him forever in a secret, sudden departure we now call the Rapture.

And though we can look back and see hints of His plan all through the Old Testament, (**Isaiah 49:6** for example) neither Satan, the leaders of Israel, nor even the Lord's closest disciples realized that His death on the cross was intended to accomplish all this.

"None of the rulers of this age understood it," Paul wrote, *"For if they had they would not have crucified the Lord of Glory."* (**1 Cor. 2:8**)

Implicit in the phrase "rulers of this age" is a reference to Satan, whom Paul called "the god of this age" in **2 Cor. 4:4**. If Satan had known that his efforts to defeat the Lord by killing Him would result in his own total defeat, he would have done anything he could to prevent it.

I've Got A Secret

For these reasons the Rapture of a largely Gentile Church had to be kept secret. It was part of God's secret wisdom, Paul said, a wisdom that has been hidden and that God destined for our glory before time began (**1 Cor 2:7**). Paul was not authorized to reveal this until nearly 20 years after the Lord's death, when it was too late for anyone to do anything about it, but it's what he meant when he wrote to the Colossians, *"And having disarmed the powers and authorities* (by paying the penalty for our sins) *He made a public spectacle of them, triumphing over them by the cross."* (**Col. 2:15**).

(It's easy to forget that up until Peter's vision and subsequent visit to the home of Cornelius detailed in **Acts 10**, most believers had come from among the Jews. The acceptance of Gentiles into the Church didn't become official policy until the council at Jerusalem 13 years after that in **Acts 15**.)

What was to have been Satan's great victory has resulted in his total defeat. Now the only ones on his side of the ledger will be those who choose to be there by rejecting God's offer of pardon. Their choice relieves God of the responsibility. He still grieves over them, but can't override their sovereign right to choose their own destiny. And since they've chosen to join him, Satan can't use them as leverage to get a better deal for himself.

The enormity of God's Gift of Grace, made available to Jew and Gentile alike and sealed with the indwelling presence of the Holy Spirit, is something so unbelievable that neither Paul nor any other Apostle was ever able to adequately describe it. The best Paul could do was to borrow a passage from Isaiah, *"No eye has seen, no ear has heard, no mind has conceived what God has prepared for those who love Him"* (**1 Cor. 2:9**). Amen to that.

And so one day soon, with no prior warning and at a time when the world least expects Him, *the Lord Himself will come down from heaven, with a loud command, with the voice of the archangel and with the trumpet call of God, and the dead in Christ will rise first. After that, we who are still alive and are left will be caught up together with them in the clouds to meet the Lord in the air. And so we will be with the Lord forever.* (**1 Thes. 4:16-17**)

There is no preceding condition, nothing that must happen first, except that if you want to be included you have to give your heart to Him who's coming before the trumpet call sounds. Better do it right away, for if you listen carefully you can almost hear the footsteps of the Messiah.

Appendix 6

Defending The Pre-Trib Rapture Of The Church

S ome body asked me a great question the other day. "Does Scripture actually promise a Pre-Tribulation Rapture, or is it just an opinion passed along from teacher to student?" Then he challenged me to cite even one Bible verse that would lead a person to believe the Pre-Trib position if they hadn't already heard about it from some Bible teacher. He said that in all his studies he's not been able to find one. Let's see if he's right.

First, Some General Points

The Rapture is not another name for the Second Coming. As **1 Thes. 4:15-17** and **John 14:1-3** explain, the Rapture is an unscheduled secret event where Jesus comes part way to Earth to meet His Church in the air and take us to be with Him where He now is. I say unscheduled and secret because its specific timing will remain unknown until it actually happens.

On the other hand, The Second Coming is a scheduled public event where Jesus comes all the way to Earth with His Church to establish a Kingdom here. I say scheduled and public because the general time of His coming will be known on Earth over 3 1/2 years in advance, and public because everyone on Earth will be able to witness His arrival. **Matt. 24:29-30** says it will happen shortly after the Great Tribulation has ended and all the nations will see the Son of Man coming on the clouds in the sky.

Membership in the Church and therefore participation in the Rapture is contingent upon having personally accepted the Lord's death as payment in full for your sins. While His death actually purchased full pardons for everyone, we each have to personally ask to have ours activated. Everyone who asks for salvation receives an unconditional, irrevocable "Yes!" (**Matt. 7:7-8, John 3:16, Ephes. 1:13-14**) For no matter how many promises God has made, they are "Yes" in Christ. (**2 Corinth. 1:20**)

It's Greek To Me

And finally, although cynics can truthfully say that the word Rapture doesn't appear in any passage of Scripture, the statement is not correct in its intent. Rapture is a word of Latin origin, not Hebrew or Greek, the languages of the Bible. (One of the earliest translations of the Bible was into Latin, and the word rapture comes from there.) Its Greek equivalent is harpazo, which is found in the Greek text of

1 Thes. 4:17. When they're translated into English, both words mean "to be caught up, or snatched away." Harpazo, the word Paul actually used, comes from roots that mean, "to raise from the ground" and" take for oneself" and hints that in doing so the Lord is eagerly claiming us for Himself. So while the Latin word doesn't appear in our Bibles, the event it describes certainly does.

There's a similar situation with the word Lucifer, also of Latin origin. It doesn't appear in any of the original texts either, but no one would be naive enough to deny the existence of Satan on such a flimsy basis. With that introduction, let's go first to the best known of the Rapture passages.

According to the Lord's own word, we tell you that we who are still alive, who are left till the coming of the Lord, will certainly not precede those who have fallen asleep. For the Lord himself will come down from heaven, with a loud command, with the voice of the archangel and with the trumpet call of God, and the dead in Christ will rise first. After that, we who are still alive and are left will be caught up together with them in the clouds to meet the Lord in the air. And so we will be with the Lord forever. (**1 Thes. 4:15-17**)

Most of us are very familiar with these verses. But notice they don't tell you when the rapture happens, only that it does. Notice also that the Lord doesn't come all the way to Earth. We meet Him in the clouds and then according to **John 14:1-3** go back with Him to where He came from. If this was the 2nd coming, He would be coming here to be where we are, not coming to take us there to be where He is.

Paul described the same event in **1 Cor 15:51-52**. In a flash, in the twinkling of an eye the dead in Christ will rise and the living will be transformed. There he said that he was disclosing a secret, but the resurrection of the dead was not a secret. It can be found through out the Old Testament. The secret was that some would not die, but would be taken alive into the Lord's presence following an instantaneous transformation. The rapture happens fast. In one instant we're walking on Earth and in the very next, we're in the Kingdom.

By the way, don't try to use the trumpet reference in verse 52 to pin the timing of the rapture to some other event. Since both the Corinthian passage and the one from Thessalonians describe the same things, it's safe to assume that the term last trump refers to the fact that the trumpet call of God from **1 Thes. 4:16** will signal the end of the Church Age, at which time the Church will disappear from Earth.

So these two references both say that one generation of humans won't die but will be suddenly changed from our earthly form to our heavenly one. And since both **Matt. 24:31** (they'll gather His elect from one end of the heavens to the other) and **Rev. 17:14** (with Him will be His called, chosen, and faithful followers) say that we'll be with the Lord when He returns, this has to happen sometime before the 2nd Coming. And it can't be just the resurrected believers coming back with Him because the Rapture passages above say that we'll be changed at the same time as the dead are raised.

So When Does This Happen?

In the New Testament, the clearest indication we get in the timing department is found in **1 Thes. 1:9-10**.

They tell how you turned to God from idols to serve the living and true God, and to wait for his Son from heaven, whom he raised from the dead—Jesus, who rescues us from the coming wrath.

The Greek word translated "from" in this passage is "apo." Taken literally, it means we're to be rescued from the time, the place, or any relation to God's wrath. It denotes both departure and separation. This is supported by **1 Thes. 5:9** that declares, *"God did not appoint us to suffer wrath but to receive salvation through our Lord Jesus Christ."*

Some folks are fond of pointing out that you can't use God's wrath interchangeably with the Great Tribulation. They're not the same, they say. And they're right, the two terms are not synonymous. The Great Tribulation is 3 1/2 years long and begins in **Rev. 11-13**. God's wrath is much longer, beginning in **Rev. 6**, as verse 17 explains. Post-trib. and pre-wrath rapture advocates try to deny this but the Scripture is clear. The time of God's wrath begins with the Seal Judgments. The Bowl Judgments that come later don't begin the time of His wrath, they conclude it. (**Rev. 15:1**) Being rescued from the time, the place and any relation to God's Wrath means the Church has to disappear before **Rev. 6**, and that's why we believe the Rapture takes place in **Rev. 4** and the Church is the group of believers in view in heaven in **Rev.5**.

You Be The Judge

Now let's apply my questioner's litmus test. Could a believer, sitting alone on the proverbial desert isle with nothing but a Bible and with no pre-conceived ideas, conclude that there's a pre-trib Rapture just from reading about it, or could he only be led into this position by first hearing someone teach him about it?

Well, From **Isaiah 13:9-13** and **Amos 5:18-20**, he would have learned that God is going to judge the Earth for it's sins in a terrible time called the Day of the Lord when He'll pour out His wrath on mankind. Reading **Matt. 24:21-22** would have told him that this time of judgment would be so bad that if the Lord didn't put a stop to it no one would survive. But the Lord will put a stop to it by returning in power and glory. Since he would know that the Lord hasn't returned yet, he would know that God's wrath is still in the future. When he got to **1 Thes. 1:9-10** he would see a pretty clear statement. Jesus rescues us from the coming wrath. In the "who, what, where, when, and why" methodology of the investigative reporter he would have the Who, (Jesus) the what, (rescues us) and the when (the time of the coming wrath).

Reading on he would come to **1 Thes. 4:15:17** and get the where (from Earth to the clouds) and in **1 Thes. 5:9** the why (because we're not appointed to wrath). From there he would logically conclude that since we'll be rescued around the time of the coming wrath and since we're not appointed to wrath, our rescue has to precede it. He could also answer another of the investigative reporter's questions in **1 Thes. 4:15:17** and that's how it would happen. The Lord himself will come down from Heaven into our atmosphere and suddenly snatch us away from Earth to join Him there. In chapter 5 he would learn that he would never know the exact timing of this event but only that it would precede the coming wrath. Of course there are many more passages I could reference but I think I've made my point and answered the question.

In fact I'll go one step further. I believe that since our hypothetical reader has no one to persuade him differently, he would assume that what he's reading is to be taken literally. And if that's the case, then the pre-trib position is the only conclusion he could logically come to, because every other position requires a moderate to massive re-interpretation of Scripture.

I contend that left alone to work this out with only the Holy Spirit as his guide he would expect to be raptured before the wrath of God begins in **Rev. 6**. You see, God didn't write the Bible to confuse us, but to inform us. It's mankind that's gotten everything all mixed up. If you give the Holy Spirit a clear minded student, uncontaminated by man's opinions and prejudices, He would bring that person to the understanding of the rapture that's most consistent with a literal interpretation of Scripture. And that requires a pre-trib rapture.

But Wait, There's More

While we're on the topic, there's another issue that points to a pre-trib Rapture and it comes to us in the form of a clue in **1 Thes. 4:15**, right at the beginning of the Rapture passage. Verse 15 opens with the phrase *"According to the Lord's own word."* There simply is no place in the New Testament where Jesus speaks of some being resurrected and some others being transformed to meet the Lord in the air. He never said anything like that, nor does he even imply such a thing.

Those who believe they see it in **Matt. 24:40-41** first have to ignore the fact that Jesus was explaining events on Earth on the actual day of His return, which would place the Rapture after the 2nd Coming, something no one believes. They also have to ignore the fact that in **Matt. 24:40-41** both believers and non-believers are sent somewhere, believers being received unto Him, while non-believers are sent away. You have to research the Greek words translated "taken" (paralambano) and "left" (alphiemi) to realize this, but when you do you'll see that the English is misleading. No Rapture view includes the disposition of non-believers, nor does it even mention them.

By the way, this is a great example of why the literal, historical, grammatical interpretation is so important. Our Bible was mostly written in Hebrew and Greek. Every translation relies on the movement of words from one language to another. This process doesn't always produce a perfect fit, and so learned men have to make allowances for this and exercise their own judgment from time to time.

But men are not perfect. We all have our biases. When it's an important issue where you want an exact meaning it's always a good idea to double-check their work. Fortunately we have an incredible tool in the Strong's Concordance. It contains every Hebrew and Greek word in the Bible with their primary and secondary meanings, how often each word appears in the Bible and what meanings are used in each appearance. You can compare these with the meaning the translators used and see if you agree with their treatment of the passage.

By doing this with **Matt. 24:40-41**, you'll find that the primary meaning of paralambano is to receive and the primary meaning of alphiemi is to send away. People with a post-trib disposition read **1 Thes. 4:15**, and then turned to **Matt. 24:40-41** where they saw one group being "taken" and another group being "left" after the end of the Great Tribulation. Assuming that these were the Lord's own words Paul was referring to, they stopped there. They had seen what they wanted to see.

In actuality **Matt. 24:40-41** is most likely a preview of the Sheep and Goat judgment of Tribulation survivors. The word taken (received) refers to believers going live into the Kingdom, and the word left (sent away) applies to non-believers who are sent to the place prepared for the Devil and his angels. (**Matt 25:31-46**) Of course none of this pertains to our desert island reader above. The verses I used there are clear enough that they don't require any research into the original language. So he wouldn't need a Strong's Concordance, just his Bible.

What's Your Point?

So if Jesus never taught about the Rapture, to which of the "Lord's own words" was Paul referring? Some dismiss the phrase, saying that Paul was speaking of a conversation he had with the Lord that doesn't appear in Scripture. But I think we deserve a better answer than that. Remember, 1st Thessalonians was probably Paul's first written communication, undertaken in 51AD.

Depending on whose opinion you accept, Matthew's Gospel was either just being written or was still nearly 10 years away. Those who give it an early date say it was written to the Jews in Jerusalem and may even have been written in Hebrew. In any case neither it nor any other Gospel was yet in wide distribution. (Mark's Gospel, the other candidate for earliest one written, doesn't contain an equivalent to **Matt 24:40-41**.)

So if Paul was referring to Scripture, as I believe Paul was, it had to be the Old Testament. Yes, like everything else in God's plan, you'll find hints of the Rapture even in the Old Testament. Look at this passage from **Isaiah 26:19-21**.

But *your dead will live; their bodies will rise. You who dwell in the dust, wake up and shout for joy. Your dew is like the dew of the morning; the earth will give birth to her dead. Go, my people, enter your rooms and shut the doors behind you; hide yourselves for a little while until his wrath has passed by. See, the LORD is coming out of his dwelling to punish the people of the earth for their sins.*

Notice how the pronouns change from second person when God speaks of His people to third person when He speaks of the people of the Earth. It means the two groups are different. Those called "my people" are told to "enter your rooms" (the rooms of **John 14:1-3**?) because the others, called "the people of Earth" are going to be punished for their sins in a period of time called His Wrath. Sound familiar? (Note: the Hebrew word translated "go" in the phrase "Go my people" is translated "come" in some translations, recalling the command to John in **Revelation 4**, "Come up here!" But the word has another primary meaning and it's my favorite. It means vanish. "Vanish, my people!" Yes we will.)

Not by any stretch of the imagination has this passage been literally fulfilled. It's an End Times prophecy that promises a resurrection of the dead and hiding of God's people while God's Wrath is unleashed on the people of Earth for their sins. And it was written 2750 years ago. The hiding of the Jews in the desert on Earth at the beginning of the Great Tribulation (**Rev. 12:14**) cannot be considered as a fulfillment of this passage because no resurrection accompanies it. (According to **Daniel 12:2** the resurrection of Old Testament believers takes place at the end of the Great Tribulation.

Of course, no one knows for sure that this is the passage Paul referred to, but as evidence of its influ-

ence on him, let's compare it with what Paul wrote in
1 Thessalonians 4-5.

Isaiah : *But your dead will live; their bodies will rise.
You who dwell in the dust, wake up and shout for joy.
Your dew is like the dew of the morning; the earth
will give birth to her dead.*
Paul: *The dead in Christ will rise first.*

Isaiah : *Go, my people, enter your rooms and shut the
doors behind you; hide yourselves for a little while
until his wrath has passed by.*
Paul: *After that, we who are still alive and are left
will be caught up together with them in the clouds to
meet the Lord in the air.*

Isaiah : *See, the LORD is coming out of his dwelling
to punish the people of the earth for their sins.*
Paul: *While people are saying, "Peace and safety,"
destruction will come on them suddenly, as labor
pains on a pregnant woman, and they will not escape.*

The wording is a little different, but it sure looks
to me like they're describing the same event.

And Still More

There are other sound theological reasons why
the Church will be raptured before the End Times
judgments begin. One is that the Lord seems to keep
Israel and the Church separate, never dealing with
both at the same time (**Acts 15: 13-18**) If the primary
purpose of Daniel's 70th week is to finish fulfilling

the six promises to Israel in **Daniel 9:24**, then the Church has to disappear.

Another is that the Church was purified at the cross at which time all the punishment due us was born by the Lord Himself. From that time forward the Church is considered by God to be as righteous as He is (**2 Cor 5:17 & 21**) The idea that the Church needs to undergo some discipline to become worthy to dwell with God is unscriptural and denies the Lord's completed work on the cross.

And third, the stated purpose of the Great Tribulation is twofold, to purify Israel and completely destroy the unbelieving nations. (**Jeremiah 30:1-11**) The Church isn't destined for either of these outcomes.

There are also several subtle clues that on their own can't be used to support the pre-trib position, but which underscore the validity of the clear passages I've just cited. Take for instance the fact that Enoch, who bears a great similarity to the Church, disappeared before the Great Flood, that the angels couldn't destroy Sodom and Gomorrah until Lot and his family were clear, and that Daniel was missing from the story of the fiery furnace, a model of the Great Tribulation.

When the Lord described His coming in **Luke 17:26-29** He said that it would be both like the days of Noah (some will be preserved through the accompanying judgments) and the days of Lot (some will taken away before them).

And what about the promise He made to the Church in Philadelphia that he would keep us out of the "hour" of trial coming on the whole world. (**Rev. 3:10**)

But being asked to cite verses that didn't require any prior knowledge I picked two that are clearest to me, **1 Thes. 1:9-10** and **Isaiah 26: 19-21**. And so by the testimony of two witnesses, one in the Old Testament and one in the New, we see the physical separation of believers from non-believers preceding the time of Judgment. And by the testimony of two witnesses a thing shall be established. (**Deut. 19:15**) Of course some won't be convinced until we show them a verse that says the rapture will precede the Great Tribulation in those exact words. Obviously, such a verse doesn't exist. I guess we'll just have to wait and explain it to them on the way up.

Appendix 7

The Coming Temple

According to Prophecies in **Daniel 9:27, Matt 24:15** and **2 Thes 2:4**, a Temple will exist in Israel at the beginning of the Great Tribulation. This is confirmed by **Revelation 11:1** which describes John measuring a Temple before the Tribulation. Its location is the "Holy City." Chapter 11 also introduces the 2 witnesses who preach in the "Great City" and are ultimately killed there, their bodies left lying in the street. The Great City is identified as the place where the Lord was crucified: Jerusalem. But is Jerusalem also the Holy City?

According to **Zechariah 14:6-9** on the day of the Lord's return an earthquake will split the Mt. of Olives in two along an East-West line that creates a great valley through the center of Jerusalem. Immediately a river will fill the valley creating a waterway from the Mediterranean to the Dead Sea. If the Lord returns to the same area of the Mt. of

Olives from which He left, as suggested by **Acts 1:11**, the earthquake creating this East-West valley will destroy the current Temple mount and anything that may be standing upon it.

Ezekiel 47:1-12 describes a great river flowing south from under the south side of the Temple and then eastward to the Dead Sea during a period of time that most scholars believe has not occurred yet. **Revelation 22:1-2** confirms this. If as it appears, Ezekiel, Zechariah, and Revelation all describe the same river, then an interesting scenario begins to emerge.

This scenario requires a Temple to be present on the day the Lord returns, but since the current Temple mount will have been destroyed by the earthquake mentioned above, this Temple must be somewhere else. Since the river originates under the Temple and flows from its south side before heading East and West, the Temple must be north of the newly created river valley.

Where Are The 12 Tribes?

Plotting the land grants for the 12 tribes given in the 48th chapter of Ezekiel on a map of Israel places the precincts of the Holy City north of the current City of Jerusalem. This new location is the ancient City of Shiloh, where the Tabernacle stood for nearly 400 years after the Israelites first conquered the Land. This is the Holy City and its name is Jehovah Shammah according to the last verse in Ezekiel. The Hebrew translates as "the LORD is here."

This new location would meet all the requirements for the Temple mentioned in the above references. The current Temple Mount in Jerusalem would not.

According to **Ezekiel 44:6-9**, this Temple will have been defiled in a way never seen in history, therefore at a time yet future to us. A foreigner uncircumsized in heart (neither Christian) and flesh (nor Jewish) will have been given charge of the sanctuary while offering sacrifices. If we understand the chronology of Ezekiel, this event will have taken place after both the 1948 re-gathering prophesied in **36-37** and the national wake-up call prophesied in **38-39** but before the Millennial Kingdom begins. The only event we know of that fits that chronology is the Great Tribulation. This is confirmed by Paul's prophecy of **2 Thes. 2:4** where the anti-christ sets himself up in the Temple proclaiming himself to be God.

After the Second Coming it will be cleansed for use in the Millennium, just as the Macabbean Temple was cleansed for use in the time leading up to the First Coming. Some believe this cleansing will be the prophetic fulfillment of the Feast of Hanukkah.

Here then is a rough outline of events. Following Israel's return to God after the battle of **Ezekiel 38-39**, the Jewish people will re-establish their covenant (old not new) with Him. This will require a return to Levitical practices and so a Temple will be built. This is the Temple spoken of in **Daniel 9** and **Revelation 11**.

Following instructions given by Ezekiel and needing to avoid the enormous problems a Jerusalem Temple would create in the Moslem world, this Temple will be located north of Jerusalem in Shiloh. It will be defiled in the middle of the last 7 years as outlined in **Daniel 9:24-27**, **Ezekiel 44:6-9**, **Matt 24:15** and **2 Thes 2:4** kicking off the Great Tribulation, but will be cleansed by living water that begins flowing from it on the day the Lord returns (**Zech 14:8**). This temple so vividly described in **Ezekiel 40-48**, will be used during the Millennium to memorialize the Lord's work at the cross just as the Old Testament Temples looked forward to it. This is the Millennial Temple

The New Jerusalem

The Ezekiel passage also solves the Jerusalem / New Jerusalem problem. For as long as I've been studying these things, there has been debate over the issue of the New Jerusalem. Some wonder how the Lord could permit redeemed believers and unbelieving natural humans to co-exist in the Millennium. (The rotten apple spoiling the barrel theory) Others wonder how a city with a foot print 1400 miles square and tall could be located in Israel when the whole country won't be that big.

Carefully examining **Rev 21** and **22**, we notice that John never actually says the city arrives on earth. We are only told he sees it coming down out of heaven, prepared as a bride. (Not that the city IS the bride, but that as with a bride on her wedding day, no effort has been spared to make it look its absolute best.)

I don't believe the city ever rests on the Earth's surface, but rather orbits in the proximity of Earth, like a satellite or perhaps another moon. At 1400 miles square and tall it would cover half the area of the US, and be 4,000 times as tall as the world's tallest building. From a planetary perspective it would be about 2/3rds the size of the Moon. It simply would not fit anywhere on Earth.

Also comparing the descriptions of New Jerusalem with Jehovah Shammah we see some similarities but enough differences to refute the notion that John and Ezekiel described the same place. Compare the following:

New Jerusalem (All verses from Rev.)	**Jehovah Shammah** (All verses from Ezekiel)
12 gates named after Israel (21:12)	12 gates named after Israel (48:30)
12 foundations named after Apostles (21:14)	Foundation not described
1400 miles square and tall (21:16)	One mile square (48:30)
Coming Down from heaven (21:2)	Located in Israel on Earth (40:2)
No Temple ... God and the Lamb are its Temple (21:22)	Temple just north of the city (40:2)
No sin; nothing impure will ever enter (21:27)	Daily sin offerings in the Temple (45:13-15,17)

No more death (21:4)	Still death (44:25 also Isa 65:20)
No natural beings ... only the perfected (21:27)	Natural Beings (46:16)

With the differentiation of these two Holy Cities, the apparent conflict between Jewish and Christian eschatology is resolved. Israel was promised that one day GOD would come to Earth to dwell among them forever, while the Church is promised that Jesus will come to take us to heaven to live with Him there. Both promises come true.

Since Ezekiel specifically quoted the Lord's promise to dwell among the Israelites forever (**43:7**) and then described the new Holy City, while Jesus promised to return for the Church to take us to be with Him (**John 14:1-3**), they must have been talking about two different destinations. They were. Heaven is the New Jerusalem where we will dwell with the Lord forever, while the Holy City on Earth is Jehovah Shammah where God will dwell in the midst of His people Israel forever.

CPSIA information can be obtained at www.ICGtesting.com
Printed in the USA
LVOW082110211012

303825LV00001B/10/P

9 781619 043985